Get me out of the Kitchen!

COOKBOOK

BY SHARON AND GENE McFALL

Creative Ideas Publishing

Contents

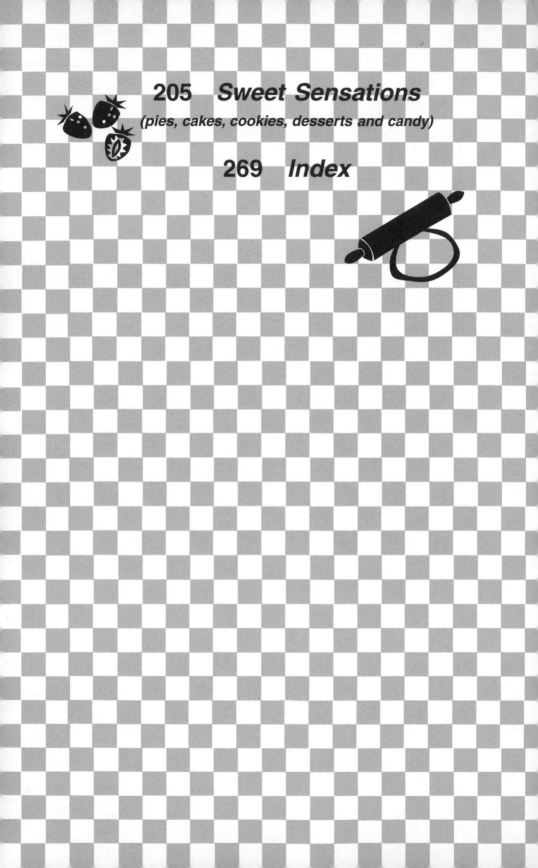

Acknowledgments

The creation of a successful cookbook requires many things: creating, collecting and testing recipes, research for tips, hints and other material, and time and money. It also requires the efforts of many talented people.

We would like to express our appreciation to all the wonderful people who donated their favorite recipies to this cookbook.

About the Authors

Get Me Out of the Kitchen *is the third cookbook the husband and wife team of Sharon and Gene McFall have co-authored. Others are the beautiful and interesting* Cookin' With Will *and the national best seller,* Busy Woman's Cookbook.

SHARON MCFALL is a native of Des Moines, Iowa. In recent years she has traveled extensively in the U.S. and around the world. She has coordinated major seminars for working women, owned and operated a restaurant and concessions at Renfro Valley Country Music Center, designed and developed gift shops and women's apparel shops in important tourist areas and was vice-president of operations for a dinner theatre. She is the mother of two sons and two daughters and she has three granddaughters and two grandsons. When not writing Sharon promotes the cookbooks and her husband's Will Rogers show. She now lives in Edmond, Oklahoma, only ten minutes from her granddaughters.

GENE MCFALL has performed his renowned role of Will Rogers in 45 states and around the world since 1982. He was James Whitmore's understudy and performed "Will Rogers' U.S.A." for seven years, then in 1989 wrote his own one-man show, "Witty World of Will Rogers." Gene was cast as Will Rogers in the public television miniseries, "Oklahoma Passage." As Will, Gene has drawn praise for his performances before Will Rogers' sons, President George H. Bush, Supreme Court Justice Byron White, UN Ambassador Jean Kirkpatrick, scores of U.S. Senators and Congressmen, Governors and lawmakers, and in stage shows and conventions. As a special staff member of the Will Rogers Memorial Museum for five years, Gene performed a special program on Will Rogers for nearly half a million students in Oklahoma.

Introduction

Today's fast-paced life makes inumerable demands on the modern woman's time. If she is a mother, her children are involved in school activities, after school functions (and in some cases, before school programs), for which she must act as a chauffer, adult supervisor, or just as a spectator.

The career woman-whether married or single-must contend with the pressures of today's competitive work place. She is expected to work the necessary hours, keep up on all the advances in her field, be stylishly dressed and groomed, and handle the stress of her job with a smile and without complaint.

If she is married she is expected to be very interested in her husband's career, be a witty, well-informed companion at his company's social functions and a charming hostess if he entertains clients or associates.

In the home she is expected to be a professional decorator, balancing a stylish look with the utilitarian needs of her family. And who do you think is expected to keep the mountains of laundry done? At least, thank God for permanent press!

And finally, what about food? There are two or three fast food places on nearly every corner, and a sit-down restaurant at least every two blocks. But how many burgers or tacos or pizzas can you eat before your taste buds say, "That's enough." What about nutrition?

There is something intrinsically satisfying about a home cooked meal. It offers one of the few opportunities in our hustle-bustle society for the family to function as a unit. But no one has the time to spend hours in the kitchen, no matter how strong her domestic urges are. In previous generations women expected to spend a good portion of their day in the kitchen cooking three meals a day, preparing dishes from scratch that took hours. It is possible to cook great tasting meals that will please everyone without spending hours in the kitchen. *Get Me Out Of The Kitchen* was written for that express purpose.

Each recipe requires only a small number of ingredients

most of which you will already have in your cupboard. You will not have to go to the market for 15 or 20 ingredients to make one recipe. Preparation time is minimal for each dish—you can prepare a soup or salad, a main dish, and a dessert without sacrificing a great amount of your valuable time.

Get Me out Of The Kitchen contains over 500 delicious recipes from appetizers through all the courses of a meal. Throughout the book are dozens of helpful cooking hints.

Not For Women Exclusively! A tremendous number of men cook. Their work schedule is such that they can take the responsibility for at least part of the family's meals. Also many men enjoy cooking. It is a great change of pace from their daily demands. There is satisfaction in a tasty meal home prepared-but with not a tremendous investment of time. Men will find *Get Me Out Of the Kitchen* the perfect cookbook.

But even if you are a stay-at-home person and have lots of time, do you want to spend most of it cooking? Sure there are times when you will spend hours making that gourmet meal—but do you want to do that every day? *Get Me Out Of The Kitchen* will keep your "Good Cook" reputation intact on a daily basis without the herculean effort. It will become your most used cookbook.

Let the Party Begin

(Beverages, Spreads, Dips, and Appetizers)

ORANGE JUICE SHAKE

½ cup cold milk

½ cup orange juice

2 cups vanilla ice cream

½ teaspoon vanilla extract

Combine all ingredients in blender, cover, blend until smooth. Pour mixture into chilled glasses. Makes 3 servings.

PEACHES AND CREAM MILK SHAKE

1 cup milk, divided

1 cup sliced peaches

1 pint peach ice cream

¼ cup sugar

Peach slices for garnish

Place ¼ cup of the milk and peaches in blender, cover, blend until smooth. Add ice cream and blend until softened. Add ¾ cup of the milk and the sugar and blend well. Pour into tall glasses. Garnish each serving with peach slices. Makes 4 servings.

CHOCOLATE SHAKE FOR TWO

¾ cup milk

3 tablespoons chocolate flavored syrup

1 pint vanilla ice cream

Combine milk and chocolate syrup in a blender, cover, blend untill smooth. Add half the ice cream; blend until smooth. Add the rest of the ice cream;. blend slightly. Makes 2 servings.

SUPER YOGURT SHAKE

2 cups cold milk

*1 (4 serving) box strawberry
   flavored gelatin*

1 cup plain yogurt

1 cup crushed ice

1 large banana, cut into chunks

Combine all ingredients in blender, cover, blend on high speed until smooth. Makes 4 servings.

● ●

STRAWBERRY YOGURT SHAKE

*1 (10 ounce) package frozen
   strawberries, thawed*

1 cup milk

2 cups strawberry yogurt

Place strawberries and milk into blender, cover, blend until smooth. Spoon a serving of yogurt into each of 3 tall glasses. Add the rest of the yogurt to strawberry mixture in the blender. Blend until smooth. Pour over yogurt in glasses. Serve with spoons and straws. Makes 3 servings.

TO KEEP POPCORN, POTATO CHIPS, AND OTHER MUNCHIES FRESH, STORE THEM IN THE FREEZER UNTIL READY TO EAT.

CINNAMON SPICY CIDER

4 cups apple cider

½ cup red cinnamon candies

In a medium saucepan, combine cider and candies. Stir over medium heat until candies melt and cider is hot. Makes 4 servings.

• •

ONE CUP ORANGE CIDER DRINK

1 cup apple cider

1½ teaspoons orange flavored breakfast drink powder

Dash nutmeg

Dash cinnamon

Combine all ingredients in a small saucepan. Cook and stir over medium heat until hot. Makes 1 serving.

TO CLEAN COOKING SPILLS IN YOUR OVEN, SPRINKLE SALT ON IT IMMEDIATELY AND FINISH BAKING. THE SPILLOVER WILL TURN TO ASH WHEN THE OVEN COOLS AND CAN BE REMOVED EASILY.

CROCKPOT WASSAIL

2 quarts apple juice

1 pint cranberry juice

¾ cup sugar

2 cinnamon sticks

1 teaspoon allspice

5 whole cloves

1 small orange

In a large crockpot, combine apple juice, cranberry juice, and sugar. Mix well. Add cinnamon sticks and allspice. Poke cloves into orange and place in juice mixture. Cook on high for 1 hour, then low for 4 to 8 hours. Serve hot. Makes 6 servings.

● ●

FROTHY EGGNOG

4 eggs

⅓ cup sugar

⅛ teaspoon salt

⅛ teaspoon nutmeg

2 tablespoons lemon juice

4 cups milk

½ cup cream

Super-Fast

In a medium bowl, beat eggs until thick and lemon colored. Add sugar, salt, nutmeg, lemon juice, milk, and cream. Beat with mixer until frothy. Makes 4 servings.

ORANGE JUICE SLUSH

1 cup milk

1 cup water

¾ cup orange juice

½ cup sugar

1 teaspoon vanilla

Crushed ice in 2 glasses

Combine all ingredients (except ice) in blender, cover, blend until smooth. Pour over crushed ice. Makes 2 servings.

• •

FRESH LEMONADE SERVES ONE, ME!

2 tablespoons sugar

2 tablespoons fresh squeezed lemon juice

1 cup cold water

In a small bowl, combine all ingredients. Serve over glass of ice. Makes 1 serving.

• •

ICE CREAM PUNCH

Super-Fast

1½ gallons vanilla ice cream

4 cups orange juice

½ cup lemon juice

2 (28 ounce) bottles lemon-lime soda, chilled

Spoon ice cream into a punch bowl. Add orange juice and lemon juice. Stir slowly. Add lemon-lime beverage, stirring gently. Punch will be foamy. Makes 24 servings.

TIME TO PARTY PUNCH

2 cups sugar

1½ cups water

1 cup lemon juice

1 cup orange juice

1 (6 ounce) can frozen pineapple juice, thawed

2 quarts ginger ale, chilled

In a medium saucepan, boil sugar and water for 10 minutes. Remove from heat. Stir in lemon juice, orange juice, and pineapple juice. Refrigerate until chilled. Just before serving, combine with ginger ale. Makes 16 to 20 servings.

• •

CHERRY SLUSH PUNCH

4 cups sugar

4 cups boiling water

3 (4 serving) boxes cherry flavored gelatin

9 cups boiling water

1 tablespoon almond extract

2 (28 ounce) bottles, ginger ale

In a medium saucepan, dissolve sugar in 4 cups boiling water. In a separate saucepan, dissolve gelatin in 9 cups of boiling water. Combine gelatin and sugar mixes, almond extract, and ginger ale. Refrigerate until chilled. Makes 3 gallons.

FROSTY CAPPUCCINO

1 cup cold strong coffee

2 cups fat-free vanilla ice cream

2 tablespoons chocolate flavored syrup

Place all ingredients in a blender. Cover and blend until smooth. Makes 4 servings.

Per Serving: Calories-95, Protein-3 gm, Fat-0 gm, Carbohydrates-24 gm, Cholesterol-0 mg, Sodium-55 mg.

WAKE-UP BREAKFAST SHAKE

1 cup vanilla low-fat yogurt

½ cup frozen raspberries

¼ cup orange juice

1 medium banana, cut into chunks

Place all ingredients in a blender. Cover and blend on high until smooth. Makes 2 servings.

Per Serving: Calories-215, Protein-6 gm, Fat-1 gram, Carbohy-drates-49 gm, Cholesterol-2 mg, Sodium-55 mg.

HEALTHY ORANGE COOLER

½ cup unsweetened orange juice

½ cup pear juice

1 tablespoon lemon juice

Ice cubes

Pour fruit juices and lemon juice over ice in a large glass. Makes 1 serving.

Per Serving: Calories-100, Protein-1 gram, Fat-0 gm, Carbohy-drates-24 gm, Cholesterol-0 mg, Sodium-5 mg.

CREAMY ORANGE FROST

½ cup orange juice

½ banana, mashed

1 tablespoon non-fat milk powder

⅛ teaspoon nutmeg

2 ice cubes

Super-Fast

Place all ingredients in a blender. Cover and blend until creamy. Makes 2 servings.

Per Serving: Calories-68, Protein-1 gram, Fat-Trace, Carbohydrates-16 gm, Cholesterol-12 mg, Sodium-12 mg.

• •

FRUITY CHILLED BEVERAGE

½ cup skim milk

¼ teaspoon coconut extract

¼ cup pineapple juice concentrate

½ banana, very ripe

4 ice cubes

Combine all ingredients in a blender. Cover and blend until creamy. Pour into chilled glasses. Makes 2 servings.

Per Serving: Calories-76, Protein-1 gram, Fat- 0 gm, Carbohydrates- 18 gm, Cholesterol-trace, Sodium-17 mg.

FOR JUICY LEMONS, ORANGES, AND GRAPEFRUITS, POP THEM IN THE MICROWAVE ON HIGH FOR ABOUT 15 SECONDS. ROLL ON THE COUNTER A COUPLE OF TIMES TO LOOSEN THE PULP AND THEN SLICE AND USE THEM IN YOUR FAVORITE RECIPE.

PEACH FROSTY

1 cup sliced peaches

1 cup peach juice

½ cup vanilla low-fat yogurt

4 ice cubes

Combine all ingredients in a blender. Cover and blend until smooth and frothy. Pour into chilled glasses. Makes 2 servings.

Per Serving: Calories-160, Protein-3 gm, Fat-1 gram, Carbohydrates-36 gm, Cholesterol-3 mg, Sodium-45 mg.

● ●

STRAWBERRY SMOOTHIE

1 ripe mango

½ cup vanilla low-fat yogurt

1 cup sliced strawberries

6 ice cubes

Peel mango and chop into small chunks. Place all ingredients in a blender. Cover and blend until smooth and frothy. Pour into chilled glasses. Makes 2 servings.

Per Serving: Calories-145, Protein-4 gm, Fat-2 gm, Carbohydrates-32 gm, Cholesterol-3 mg, Sodium-40 mg.

THICK AND CREAMY BANANA SHAKE

Super-Fast

1 cup mashed bananas

½ cup skim milk

1 cup peach nectar

Spoon mashed bananas into ice cube trays. Freeze. Place frozen bananas, milk and peach nectar into a blender. Blend on high until smooth. Serve immediatcly over ice cubes. Makes 3 servings.

Per Serving: Calories-150, Protein-29 gm, Fat-1 gram, Carbohydrates-35 gm, Cholesterol-0 mg, Sodium-30 mg.

FRUIT FLAVORED BANANA SHAKE

¾ cup fruit flavored non-fat yogurt

1 small banana

¼ cup skim milk

1 teaspoon honey

⅛ teaspoon cinnamon

Combine all ingredients in a blender. Cover and blend until smooth. Makes 1 serving.

Per Serving: Calories-190, Protein-7 gm, Fat-1 gm, Carbohydrates-42 gm, Cholesterol-0 mg, Sodium-87 mg.

CHICKEN SPREAD

2 cups cubed cooked chicken

½ cup prepared pesto

½ cup Miracle Whip®

Place all ingredients in blender. Cover and blend until smooth. Makes 2 servings.

COTTAGE CHEESE SPREAD

1 cup cottage cheese

1 (3 ounce) package cream cheese

½ cup sour cream

1 teaspoon lemon juice

Place all ingredients in blender. Cover and blend until smooth. Chill until ready to serve. Dust with paprika, if desired. Serve with chips, crackers or raw vegetable sticks.

CHIVE CHEESE SPREAD

1 (8 ounce) package cream cheese, softened

¼ cup chopped fresh chives

¼ teaspoon salt

⅛ teaspoon pepper

In a small bowl, combine all ingredients, mixing well. Chill until ready to serve. Makes 1 cup.

SURPRISE CHEESE SPREAD

1 cup grated Cheddar cheese

1 cup chopped ripe olives

1 cup chopped dried beef

1 cup mayonnaise

In a large bowl, combine all ingredients. Spread on party rye slices and put under broiler for about five minutes or until bubbly. Makes 6 servings.

• •

TUNA SPREAD

2 (6 ounce) cans tuna fish

2 (8 ounce) packages cream cheese, softened

1 tablespoon Miracle Whip®

1 tablespoon milk

⅛ teaspoon garlic salt

In a large bowl, combine all ingredients. Mix until smooth. Chill before serving. Serve with crackers, party bread or raw vegetable sticks. Makes 6 servings.

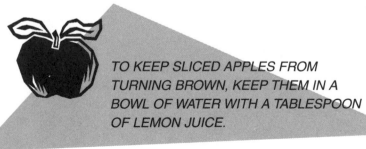

TO KEEP SLICED APPLES FROM TURNING BROWN, KEEP THEM IN A BOWL OF WATER WITH A TABLESPOON OF LEMON JUICE.

ARTICHOKE DIP

1 (6 ounce) can artichoke hearts, drained

¾ cup grated Parmesan cheese

¾ cup mayonnaise

½ teaspoon garlic powder

Preheat oven to 350 °. Place drained artichoke hearts in food processor. Add cheese, mayonnaise, and garlic powder. Mix well. Spread in 8 x 8 inch baking dish. Bake at 350° for 25 minutes. Serve with crackers. Makes 6 servings.

• •

VEGGIE SPINACH DIP

1 (10 ounce) package frozen spinach, cooked

2 cups Miracle Whip®

¼ cup cream cheese

½ cup chopped green onions

1 cup finely chopped parsley

In medium bowl, combine all ingredients. Mix well. Refrigerate 3 hours to blend flavors. Serve with vegetables. Makes 3 cups.

• •

STRAWBERRY DIP FOR FRUIT

1 cup whipped topping

1 cup strawberry yogurt

½ cup diced strawberries

In medium bowl, combine all ingredients. Mix well. Serve with fruit. Makes 2½ cups.

CREAMY CLAM DIP

Super-Fast

1 pint clams

*1 (8 ounce) package
cream cheese*

½ cup sour cream

¼ cup creamy horseradish

Preheat oven to 350°. In a medium bowl, combine all ingredients. Put in 1 quart baking dish and bake in 350° oven for 20 minutes. Makes 6 servings.

• •

CELERY SHRIMP DIP

1 (8 ounce) package cream cheese, softened

⅔ cup mayonnaise

1½ cups chopped green onions

1½ cups diced celery

1 tablespoon lemon juice

1 (6 ounce) can small shrimp, drained

In a large bowl, combine all ingredients. Refrigerate until ready to serve. Makcs 6 servings.

IMITATION CRAB DIP

Super-Fast

1 medium onion, chopped

1 stick butter

1 (10¾ ounce) can cream of mushroom soup

1 (12 ounce) package cream cheese, softened

¾ pound imitation crab

In a medium saucepan, saute onion in butter. Add soup and cream cheese. Blend well. Fold in crab meat. Serve hot. Makes 8 servings.

• •

MEATY QUESO DIP

1 pound pork sausage

¾ pound ground beef

1 (8 ounce) box Velveeta® cheese

1 (8 ounce) jar mild salsa sauce

1½ cups diced Ro-Tel® tomatoes

In a large skillet, brown sausage and ground beef. Drain on paper towel to remove fat. Combine meats, cheese, salsa, and tomatoes in a crockpot. Heat for 1 hour on high. Serve with chips. Makes 12-15 servings.

CHEESY MEXICAN DIP

Super-Fast

1 pound ground beef, cooked

1 (15 ounce) can no bean chili

½ cup sour cream

*1 (8 ounce) package Mexican-style Velveeta®
   cheese*

In a medium saucepan, combine all ingredients and cook
over low heat until cheese melts and all ingredients are
well blended. Stir constantly to avoid burning.

• •

CROCKPOT HOT CHEESE DIP

1 cup Ro-Tel® tomatoes

1 (8 ounce) package Velveeta® cheese

1 (8 ounce) package cream cheese

1 pound Cheddar cheese, shredded

Pour tomatoes into crockpot. Add cheeses. Cook on high,
stirring frequently, until cheese melts. Serve with crackers
or chips. Makes 18 servings.

*TO REMOVE ANY STINGING YOU'VE
RECEIVED FROM HANDLING HOT
PEPPERS, POUR RUBBING ALCOHOL
OVER YOUR HANDS*

GREAT FOR DIPPING CHIPS

2 pounds ground beef

1 medium onion, chopped

1 (16 ounce) jar cheese spread

1 (8 ounce) jar salsa

In a large skillet, brown ground beef and onion. Drain on paper towels to remove fat. Pour meat mixture, cheese, and salsa into crockpot. Cook on high until mixture is hot. Stir frequently. Serve hot with chips or assorted raw vegetables. Makes 10 servings.

• •

SUPER BOWL DIP

1 (8 ounce) package cream cheese, softened

½ cup mayonnaise

⅓ cup horseradish sauce

¼ cup chopped green onion

2 slices bacon, cooked and crumbled

In a medium bowl, combine cream cheese, mayonnaise, and horseradish until well blended. Fold in green onion and bacon. Mix well. Serve with chips or raw vegetables. Makes 6 servings.

• •

FRESH FRUIT DIP

2 (8 ounce) packages cream cheese, softened

⅛ teaspoon ginger

1 pint marshmallow cream

In a large bowl, combine all ingredients and mix well. Serve with sliced fresh fruit. Makes about 4 cups.

SOME LIKE IT HOT SALSA

1 (16 ounce) can stewed tomatoes

4 tomatoes, chopped

3 small jalapeno peppers, seeded and chopped

⅓ cup chopped onion

½ teaspoon salt

½ teaspoon cayenne pepper

Combine all ingredients in a blender, cover, chop until well mixed. Refrigerate until ready to serve. Makes 3 cups.

NOTE: With jalapeno seeds, the more you use, the hotter the salsa.

QUICK AND EASY SALSA

Super-Fast

6 medium tomatoes, peeled and chopped

½ cup chopped green chiles

3 jalapeno peppers, seeded and diced

⅓ cup chopped onion

1 teaspoon salt

1 clove garlic, minced

Combine all ingredients in a blender, cover, process to desired consistency. Makes 2 cups.

CREAMY GUACAMOLE

3 medium ripe avocados, mashed

1 tablespoon diced onion

¼ teaspoon salt

⅓ cup mayonnaise

1 small tomato, diced

Dash of lemon juice

Combine all ingredients. Serve immediately. Makes 2 cups.

GUACAMOLE FROM SCRATCH

2 large ripe avocados

Juice of 1 lemon

¼ cup diced red onion

3 cloves garlic, minced

1 teaspoon chili powder

In a medium bowl, mash avocado with a fork. Add lemon juice, onion, garlic, and chili powder, stirring gently. Serve immediately. Makes 1½ cups.

TO KEEP CHEESE FROM BECOMING MOLDY, SPREAD THE CUT SIDE WITH BUTTER OR MARGARINE AND THEN STORE IN A SEALED PLASTIC BAG IN THE REFRIGERATOR.

DRIED BEEF CHEESE BALL

1 (8 ounce) package cream cheese, softened

½ cup shredded Cheddar cheese

½ cup finely chopped green onion

1 (2¼ ounce) jar dried beef, finely chopped

In a medium bowl, combine all ingredients. Chill until firm. Shape into a ball and serve with crackers. Makes 8 servings.

PARTY HAM CHEESE BALL

2 (8 ounce) packages cream cheese, softened

1 bunch green onions, chopped

12 ounces shaved ham, chopped

2 teaspoons Accent® flavoring

½ teaspoon Worcestershire sauce

In a large bowl, combine all ingredients using an electric mixer on low speed. Chill until firm. Roll into a ball. Serve with crackers. Makes 12 servings.

PEPPERONI CHEESE BALL

2 (8 ounce) packages cream cheese, softened

2 (8 ounce) cans crushed pineapple, drained

2 tablespoons minced dried onion

1 tablespoon seasoning salt

3½ ounces pepperoni, finely chopped

1 cup pecans, crushed

Using a fork, combine cream cheese, pineapple, onions, salt, and pepperoni. Refrigerate until firm. Shape into a ball and roll in chopped pecans. Makes 10 servings.

• •

BAKED SAUSAGE CHEESE BALLS

2 pounds sausage

1½ cups Bisquick® mix

½ teaspoon garlic powder

4 cups shredded Cheddar cheese

½ cup diced onion

Preheat oven to 375°. In a large bowl, combine all ingredients. Form into 1 inch balls. Place on ungreased cookie sheet. Bake at 375° for 15 minutes. Serve warm. Makes about 24.

MIX AND ROLL CHEESE BALL

1 (8 ounce) package cream cheese, softened

1 (2½ ounce) package dried beef, chopped

1 tablespoon mayonnaise

3 green onions, chopped

1 tablespoon milk

⅛ teaspoon Worcestershire sauce

1 cup pecans or walnuts, crushed

In a large bowl, combine cream cheese, beef, mayonnaise, onion, milk, and Worcestershire. Mix well. Chill until firm. Form into a ball and roll in nuts. Keep refrigerated until ready to serve. Makes 6-8 servings.

• •

GARLIC CHEESE BALL

2 (8 ounce) packages cream cheese, softened

1 roll garlic cheese

½ bunch green onions, chopped

1 red bell pepper, chopped

1 cup chopped pecans

In a large bowl, combine cream cheese, garlic cheese, onion, and pepper. Mix well. Chill until firm. Roll cheese mixture into a ball and roll in finely chopped pecans. Refrigerate until ready to serve. Makes 8-10 servings.

CHEESY FRIES

Super-Fast

*1 (24 ounce) package frozen
    French fries*

2 cups shredded Cheddar cheese

1 (4 ounce) can bacon bits

Ranch dressing

Bake French fries according to package directions.
Remove from oven. Sprinkle cheese and bacon bits over
fries. Return to oven and bake until cheese melts. Serve
with Ranch dressing for dipping. Makes 8 servings.

• •

FAST CHEESY BREAD STICKS

⅓ cup Miracle Whip®

¼ cup grated Parmesan cheese

½ teaspoon Italian seasoning

3 hot dog buns, split

In a small bowl, mix Miracle Whip®, Parmesan cheese, and
Italian seasoning. Stir until well blended. Spread mixture
on cut side of each hot dog bun. Slice each half lengthwise.
Arrange on broiler pan. Broil until golden brown. Makes 3
or 4 servings.

*FRESHEN SLIGHTLY STALE BREAD, DOUGHNUTS,
OR BISCUITS, BY PLACING THEM IN A WIDE
MOUTH JAR WITH A DAMP PAPER TOWEL.
CLOSE THE LID AND
LEAVE OVERNIGHT.*

SAUCY CHICKEN WINGS

8 chicken wings

½ cup ketchup

¼ cup diced onion

1 tablespoon honey

1 tablespoon vinegar

1 clove garlic, minced

Preheat oven to 375°. Rinse chicken; pat dry. Remove and discard wing tips. Cut each wing at the joint to make two sections. Place wings in a single layer in a 13 x 9 x 2 inch baking pan. Bake at 375° for 20 minutes. Remove from oven. Pour liquid from pan. Mix ketchup, onion, honey, vinegar, and garlic. Pour over wings. Return to oven for 10 minutes. Makes 16.

BITE SIZED PIZZA

Super-Fast

2 (10 count) cans flaky biscuits

1 (16 ounce) jar pizza sauce

1 (10 ounce) package pepperoni slices

½ cup grated Parmesan cheese

1 (10 ounce) package shredded mozzarella cheese

Preheat oven to 400°. Separate each biscuit into four layers. Place biscuit layers on cookie sheet. Top each layer with 1 teaspoon sauce and 2 pieces pepperoni. Sprinkle with Parmesan and mozzarella cheese. Bake at 400° for 6 to 8 minutes or until cheese melts. Makes 24 servings.

QUICK STEP SHRIMP KABOBS

24 cooked cheese filled spinach tortellini

½ cup Italian dressing

12 medium cooked peeled deveined shrimp

12 small cherry tomatoes

In small bowl, combine dressing, tortelline, shrimp, and tomatoes. Cover and refrigerate 1 hour. Drain mixture. Thread tortellini, shrimp and tomatoes on each of twelve 6-inch skewers. Makes 12 Kabobs.

• •

OLD TIME DEVILED EGGS

6 hard cooked eggs

½ teaspoon salt

¼ teaspoon mustard

2 tablespoons pickle relish

3½ tablespoons Miracle Whip®

1 tablespoon sugar

Peel eggs and cut in half. Slip out yolks. Place yolks in small bowl and mash with fork. Add salt, mustard, relish, Miracle Whip®, and sugar, mix well. Fill whites with yolk mixture. Makes 6 to 10 servings.

TAMALE HORS D'OEUVRES

Super-Fast

2 (15 ounce) cans tamales

1 (16 ounce) can no bean chili

1 (8 ounce) jar salsa

2 (5 ounce) jars Old English cheese spread

1 onion, chopped

Chop tamales into bite sized pieces. In a large bowl, combine tamale pieces, chili, salsa, cheese, and onion. Place in crockpot and keep warm. Pour over a bed of chips in small bowls, or serve with crackers for dipping. Makes 12 servings.

• •

TASTY OYSTER CRACKERS

1 (10 ounce) bag oyster crackers

1 cup vegetable oil

1 (1 ounce) package Ranch dressing mix

1 teaspoon dill

1 teaspoon garlic powder

Preheat oven to 275°. Spread crackers on a cookie sheet. Mix oil, dressing mix, dill, and garlic powder. Pour over crackers. Bake at 275° until crackers are brown. (About 10 minutes). Makes 4 cups.

RINSE YOUR MAYONNAISE JAR WITH VINEGAR BEFORE REUSING IT. THE VINEGAR TAKES AWAY THE MAYONNAISE ODOR.

RANCH PARTY PRETZELS

1 (20 ounce) package large thick pretzels

1 (1 ounce) package Ranch dressing mix

¾ cup vegetable oil

1½ teaspoons dill

1½ teaspoons garlic powder

Preheat oven to 250 °. Break pretzels into bite sized pieces and place in a large bowl. Combine Ranch dressing, oil, dill, and garlic powder and pour over pretzels. Stir to coat. Pour into an ungreased 15 x 10 inch baking pan. Bake at 250° for 1 hour, stirring every 15 minutes. Makes 3 cups.

• •

HOMEMADE CRACKER JACKS

1 cup butter

2 cups brown sugar

½ cup light corn syrup

½ teaspoon baking soda

1 teaspoon vanilla extract

6 to 8 quarts popped corn

Preheat oven to 250°. In a large saucepan, combine butter, sugar, and syrup. Boil for 3 minutes. Remove from heat. Stir in soda and vanilla. Pour mixture over popcorn, mixing well. Place popcorn in buttered baking pans and bake at 250° for 45 minutes, stirring often. Remove from oven. Stir until cool. Makes 6-8 quarts.

BAGEL CHIPS

Super-Fast

1 package plain bagels
½ cup butter
¼ teaspoon garlic salt

Preheat oven to 400°. Slice the bagels as thinly as possible. Place bagel slices on an ungreased cookie sheet. Melt butter and stir in garlic salt. Using a pastry brush, brush each bagel slice with seasoned butter. Bake at 400° for 10-15 minutes or until toasted. Serve with chive cheese. Makes 60 to 80 chips.

● ●

NUTS SURPRISE

¼ cup butter
2 cups walnuts
1 tablespoon sugar
¼ teaspoon allspice
½ teaspoon cinnamon

In a medium saucepan, melt butter and add nuts. Cook and stir over low heat for two minutes. Add sugar and spices. Mix until well coated. Cool on cookie sheet. Makes 2 cups.

TO REMOVE ONION ODOR FROM YOUR SKIN, WET IT AND THEN RUB IN SALT. RINSE AND WASH WITH SOAP AND THE ODOR WILL BE GONE.

APPLE DELIGHTS

1 (8 ounce) package cream cheese, softened

¾ cup packed brown sugar

1 teaspoon vanilla extract

6 apples, cut into wedges

1 cup chopped peanuts

In a small bowl, beat cream cheese, brown sugar, and vanilla until smooth. Spread mixture over apple wedges. Top with nuts. Makes 6 servings.

DIPPY STIX FRUIT DIP

Super-Fast

1 (8 ounce) package cream cheese with strawberries

1 (7 ounce) jar marshmallow cream

2 tablespoons orange juice

In a large bowl, mix all ingredients until smooth. Serve with fruit skewered on wooden toothpicks. Makes 1½ cups.

TO MAKE LIMP CELERY CRISP, PLACE IT IN A BOWL OF COLD WATER WITH A SLICED POTATO AND LET STAND FOR AN HOUR OR SO.

PIMIENTO CHEESE SPREAD

Super-Fast

1 (2 ounce) jar minced pimientos

1 cup low-fat cottage cheese, drained

1 tablespoon salsa

1 teaspoon chopped chives

In a small bowl, combine all ingredients until smooth. Makes 1 cup.

Per Serving (1 tablespoon): Calories-14, Protein-2 gm, Fat-trace, Carbohydrates-1 gm, Cholesterol-<1 mg, Sodium-59 mg.

APRICOT DIPPING SAUCE

1 cup apricot jam

½ teaspoon orange zest

¼ cup orange juice

1 teaspoon dry mustard

2 tablespoons white vinegar

1 teaspoon reduced sodium soy sauce

In a medium saucepan, combine all ingredients. Cook until mixture is hot and bubbly. Serve warm. Great for dipping chicken fingers. Makes 1¼ cup.

Per Serving: Calories-58, Protein-0.2 gm, Fat-0.1 gm, Carbohy-drates-15.4 gm, Cholesterol-0 mg, Sodium-35.8 mg.

WONDERFUL FRUIT DIP

½ cup nonfat vanilla yogurt

½ cup reduced-fat frozen whipped topping

4 teaspoons reduced calorie pancake syrup

⅛ teaspoon cinnamon

In a medium bowl, combine all ingredients. Cover and refrigerate before serving. Great with fresh fruit. Makes 1 cup.

Per Serving: Calories-22, Protein-trace, Fat- 1 gram, Carbohydrates- 3 gm, Cholesterol- trace, Sodium-16 mg.

NO FAT CHOCOLATE FRUIT DIP

Super-Fast

1 cup nonfat vanilla yogurt

½ cup packed brown sugar

1 tablespoon cocoa

½ teaspoon vanilla extract

⅛ teaspoon cinnamon

In a small bowl, combine all ingredients. Beat until smooth. Chill before serving. Serve with assorted fresh fruit.

Per Serving: Calories-40, Protein-1 gram, Fat-0 gm, Carbohydrates-9 gm, Cholesterol-0 mg, Sodium-20 mg.

PINEAPPLE AND VANILLA YOGURT DIP

1 cup nonfat vanilla yogurt

¼ cup flaked coconut

2 tablespoons packed brown sugar

1 (8 ounce) can crushed pineapple, drained

In a medium bowl, combine all ingredients. Cover and refrigerate 1 hour. Serve with fresh fruit or cheese cubes. Makes 2 cups.

Per Serving: Calories-15, Protein-0 gm, Fat-0 gm, Carbohydrates-2 gm, Cholesterol-0 mg, Sodium-5 mg.

• •

CREAMY ONION DIP

½ cup low-fat plain yogurt

*1 packet instant onion broth and
    seasoning mix*

2 teaspoons chopped chives

In a small bowl, combine all ingredients. Mix until smooth. Cover and chill before serving. Makes 4 servings.

Per Serving: Calories-21, Protein-2 gm , Fat-0.4 gm, Carbohydrates-2 gm, Cholesterol-2 mg, Sodium-211 mg.

TO TAKE AWAY THE PAIN FROM A BEE STING, APPLY A SLICE OF ONION TO THE AFFECTED AREA.

TORTILLA CHIPS DIP

1 (16 ounce) can fat-free refried beans

1 cup low-fat sour cream

1 packet taco seasoning

1 cup salsa

1 cup shredded low-fat Cheddar cheese

1 tomato, diced

Spread refried beans in a 9 inch glass pie plate. In a small bowl, combine sour cream and taco seasoning. Spread over beans. Top with salsa. Evenly sprinkle cheese and tomatoes over salsa. Serve with baked tortilla chips. Makes 8 servings.

Per Serving: Calories-131, Protein-8 gm , Fat-4 gm, Carbohydrates-15 gm, Cholesterol-16 mg, Sodium-648 mg.

SALSA BEAN DIP

Super-Fast

1 (16 ounce) can kidney beans

⅛ teaspoon ground cumin

1 garlic clove, minced

½ cup no-salt tomato paste

½ small onion, finely chopped

2 tablespoons no-salt hot salsa

In a blender, combine beans, cumin, garlic, and tomato paste. Mix well. Pour into small bowl. Fold in onion and salsa. Makes 1 cup.

Per Serving: Calories-15, Protein-trace, Fat-trace, Carbohydrates-2.8 gm, Cholesterol-0 mg, Sodium-20.7 mg.

TOMATILLO SALSA

¼ cup chopped onion

2 Tablespoons cilantro

2 Tablespoons shredded watercress

1 teaspoon vegetable oil

¼ teaspoon salt

½ pound tomatillos, cut in half

1 or 2 green chiles, seeded

Place all ingredients in a blender. Cover and blend until smooth. Pour into a small bowl and refrigerate before serving. Makes 1 cup.

Per Serving (1 tablespoon): Calories-10, Protein-0 gm , Fat-0 gm, Carbohydrates-1 gram, Cholesterol-0 mg, Sodium-35 mg.

FAVORITE NACHOS SUPREME

Super-Fast

Half of a 10 ounce bag baked
 tortilla chips

¼ cup sliced black olives

¼ cup chopped onion

½ cup salsa

1 cup shredded low-fat Cheddar cheese

Evenly spread tortilla chips on a cookie sheet. Sprinkle chips with olives and onion. Top with salsa. Sprinkle with cheese. Broil 2 minutes or until cheese melts. Makes 6 servings.

Per Serving: Calories-158, Protein-8 gm, Fat-5 gm, Carbohydrates-21 gm, Cholesterol-13 mg, Sodium-341 mg.

APPETIZER MEATBALLS

1 pound ground beef

½ cup chopped onion

1 egg

⅓ cup dry bread crumbs

¼ cup milk

Salt and pepper to taste

1 (17 ounce) jar salsa

2 green onions

Preheat oven to 400°. In a large bowl, combine ground beef, onion, egg, bread crumbs, milk, salt, and pepper. Mix well. Shape into 1 inch balls. Mixture will make about 30 meatballs. Place in an ungreased 13 x 9 inch baking pan. Bake at 400° for 15 to 20 minutes. Remove from oven. In a 2 quart saucepan, combine meatballs and salsa. Heat to boiling, stirring often. Reduce heat, cover, and simmer for 15 minutes. Pour into serving dish. Chop green onions, including tops and use as a garnish. Makes 30 appetizers.

Per Serving (1 meatball): Calories-40, Protein-3 gm, Fat-3 gm, Carbohydrates-2 gm, Cholesterol-15 mg, Sodium-70 mg.

PRETZEL STICKS MAKE GREAT PICKS FOR MEATBALL APPETIZERS.

CRISPY CRUNCH

2 tablespoons butter

1 teaspoon ground cumin

⅛ teaspood ground red pepper

2 cups cashews

1 5 ounce corn nuts

2 cups dried cherries

Melt butter in 10-inch skillet until sizzling; add cumin and red pepper. Stir in cashews and corn nuts. Cook over medium heat, stirring constantly, until lightly browned. Remove from heat. In a medium bowl place mixture, add cherries and toss to coat. Store in a tightly covered container.

Per Serving: Calories 250, Protein 5-gm, Fat-14 gm, Carbohydrates 30 gm, Cholesterol 5-mg, Sodium 220 mg.

MIX AND MATCH SNACK

Super-Fast

4 cups graham cracker cereal

2 tablespoons butter, melted

1 cup M&M's® candy

1 cup miniature marshmallows

½ cup peanuts

In a large bowl, combine cereal and butter, tossing to coat. Let stand 1 minute. Add candy, marshmallows, and peanuts, tossing to coat. Store in tightly covered container. Makes 12 servings.

Per Serving: Calories-150, Protein-2 gm, Fat-6 gm, Carbohydrates-24 gm, Cholesterol-5 mg, Sodium-150 mg.

CARAMEL SWEET POPCORN BALLS

1 tablespoon sugar

1 tablespoon caramel topping, warm

½ teaspoon vanilla extract

2 cups plain popped corn

In a small non-stick skillet, over very low heat, cook and stir sugar until it melts and turns golden. Be careful not to burn it. Add caramel and vanilla extract. Cook and stir until mixture is smooth and bubbly. Spray a medium bowl with non-stick vegetable cooking spray. Pour popcorn into bowl. Pour mixture over popcorn. Moisten your hands with cold water and shape popcorn into 4 balls.

Per Serving: Calories-95, Protein-1 gram, Fat-0.4 gm, Carbohydrates-21 gm, Cholesterol-0 mg, Sodium-0.3 mg.

Stepping It Up

(Soups, Salads, and Salad Dressings)

TUNE UP BROCCOLI CHEESE SOUP

1 (10 ounce) package frozen chopped broccoli

2 (10¾ ounce) cans cream of celery soup

2 chopped carrots

1 (8 ounce) package Velveeta® cheese, cubed

1 pint half and half milk

In large saucepan, combine all ingredients over medium heat until hot. Reduce heat to low and simmer 40 to 50 minutes. Makes 6 to 8 servings.

CHINESE EGG DROP SOUP

6 cups chicken broth

2 eggs

Salt

2 teaspoons cornstarch

¼ cup water

In a large saucepan, bring chicken broth to a boil. In a small bowl, beat eggs until lemon colored and gradually pour into boiling broth. Stir while pouring. Add salt. Dissolve cornstarch in water and pour into soup. Stir until soup thickens. Makes 4 to 6 servings.

EASY MINESTRONE SOUP

1 pound ground beef

2 (10¾ ounce) cans minestrone soup

2 (14½ ounce) cans stewed tomatoes, undrained

2 (15 ounce) cans mixed vegetables, undrained

1 (10 ounce) can Ro-Tel® tomatoes

½ cup vegetable juice

In a large skillet, brown ground beef and drain off fat. Return to pan and add soup, tomatoes, mixed vegetables, Ro-Tel®, and juice. Simmer until hot. Makes 6 to 8 servings.

• •

CREAMY MUSHROOM SOUP

2 tablespoons butter

½ cup chopped onions

¼ pound fresh mushrooms, sliced

2 tablespoons flour

Salt and pepper to taste

Milk for thickening

Melt butter and cook onion until soft, not brown. Remove onion and add sliced mushrooms, cooking gently for 5 minutes. Add cooked onion, flour, salt, and pepper; stir well. Add enough milk to thicken broth. Stir constantly until soup is smooth. Makes 4 servings.

TO REMOVE MOISTURE OR LEFT OVER SCRAPS FROM A MEAT GRINDER, RUN SEVERAL SODA CRACKERS THROUGH IT.

TO RETURN SOFT, WRINKLED POTATOES TO THEIR ORIGINAL FIRMNESS, PEEL AND SLICE THEM AND STORE IN A BOWL OF COLD WATER IN THE REFRIGERATOR OVERNIGHT.

OYSTER SOUP

4 tablespoons butter

1 pint oysters, undrained

2 cups milk

1 cup cream

Salt and pepper to taste

In a large saucepan, melt butter and add oysters and liquid. Simmer until oysters curl. Add milk, cream, salt, and pepper. Cook until hot, stirring constantly. Makes 4 servings.

NAVY BEAN SOUP

2 cups dried navy beans

4 cups water

½ stick butter

1½ cups cubed ham

Salt and pepper to taste

In a large pot, cook beans in water until tender. Add more water if needed. Just before beans are done, add butter, ham, salt, and pepper, stirring well. Makes 4 to 6 servings.

RANCH STYLE BEAN SOUP

1½ pounds ground beef

1 onion, chopped

3 (10¾ ounce) cans minestrone soup

2 (15 ounce) cans Ranch style beans

1 (10 ounce) can Ro-Tel® tomatoes

In a medium skillet, brown ground beef and onion. Drain on paper towels to remove fat. Place all ingredients in a crockpot. Cook on low for 2 hours. Makes 6 servings.

• •

POTATO AND ONION SOUP

4 medium potatoes, peeled and sliced

4 onions, chopped

3 quarts water

1 stick butter

1 quart milk

Salt and pepper to taste

In a large stew pot, boil potatoes and onions in water until tender. Add butter, milk, salt, and pepper. Cook and stir until thoroughly heated. Makes 4 to 6 servings.

WHAT AU GRATIN SOUP!

1 (5¼ ounce) package dried au gratin potatoes

1 (15 ounce) can tomatoes and green chiles

2 cups water

1 (15 ounce) can Mexican style corn, drained

1 pound Velveeta® cheese, cubed

3 cups milk

In a large saucepan, cook potatoes, tomatoes, green chiles, and water until potatoes are tender, about 20 minutes. Add corn, cheese, and milk, and heat until cheese melts. Makes 6 to 8 servings.

• •

CREAMY POTATO SOUP

3 medium potatoes, peeled and cubed

1 cup chopped onions

8 slices bacon, cooked crisp and crumbled

1 (10¾ ounce) can cream of chicken soup

1 cup sour cream

1½ cups milk

Salt and pepper to taste

In a large saucepan, place potatoes, onions, and crumbled bacon. Cover with water. Bring to a boil. Lower heat and simmer for 15 to 20 minutes. Stir in soup and sour cream. Add milk, salt, and pepper. Simmer for 5 minutes. Makes 7 cups.

NOT JUST CRANBERRY SALAD

1 (4 serving) box unflavored gelatin

1 cup boiling water

1 cup marshmallow cream

1 (16 ounce) can whole cranberry sauce

1 (8 ounce) can crushed pineapple

1 apple, chopped

½ cup chopped pecans

In a large saucepan, dissolve gelatin in water. Add marshmallow cream and mix well. Add cranberry sauce, pineapple, apple, and pecans. Mix well. Chill slightly, stirring occasionally until gelatin starts to set. Pour into serving dishes and chill until firm. Makes 6 servings.

FIX IT QUICK CRANBERRY SALAD

Super-Fast

2 (4 serving) boxes raspberry flavored gelatin

1 cup boiling water

1 (16 ounce) can whole cranberry sauce

1 (8 ounce) can crushed pineapple

2 cups miniature marshmallows

In a large saucepan, dissolve gelatin in boiling water. Cool. Fold in cranberry sauce and pineapple. Pour into serving dish. Chill until firm. Top with marshmallows. Makes 6 to 8 servings.

COOL ORANGE SALAD

1 (4 serving) box orange
  flavored gelatin

½ pint orange sherbet

1 (11 ounce) can mandarin oranges, drained

In a medium saucepan, prepare gelatin as directed on package. Add sherbet and oranges. Chill until firm. Makes 4 servings.

• •

ICE CREAM FRUIT SALAD

1 (4 serving) box orange flavored gelatin

½ pint vanilla ice cream

1 apple, chopped

1 banana, chopped

½ cup chopped pecans

In a large saucepan, prepare gelatin as directed on package. Add ice cream, apple, banana, and pecans. Mix well. Place in large bowl. Chill until firm. Makes 4 servings.

• •

ICE CREAM SALAD

1 (4 serving) box lemon flavored gelatin

1 cup boiling water

1 (8 ounce) can crushed pineapple, drained

1 quart vanilla ice cream

½ cup chopped nuts

In a large bowl, dissolve gelatin in water. Add pineapple, ice cream, and nuts, mixing well. Freeze. Makes 6 to 8 servings.

TO SHELL PECANS THE EASY WAY, FIRST PLACE THEM IN BOILING WATER FOR 15 MINUTES, LET THEM COOL AND THE SHELLS WILL CRACK RIGHT OFF.

SUPREME PEAR SALAD

1 (29 ounce) can pears, undrained
1 (4 serving) box lime flavored gelatin
1 (3 ounce) package cream cheese, softened
¾ cup whipping cream

Drain juice from pears and pour into a small saucepan. Dissolve gelatin in boiling juice. Chill until partially set. Mash pears and cream cheese. Combine gelatin and pear-cheese mixture. Whip cream until stiff. Fold into mixture. Pour into mold or serving dish. Chill until ready to serve. Serve on lettuce cups. Makes 6 to 8 servings.

• •

PINEAPPLE CARROT SALAD

1 (4 serving) box orange flavored gelatin
½ cup grated carrots
1 cup crushed pineapple, drained
2 tablespoons sugar
½ cup raisins

In a large bowl, prepare gelatin according to package directions. When gelatin begins to thicken, add carrots, pineapple, sugar, and raisins. Mix well and chill until set. Makes 4 servings.

PINEAPPLE DELIGHT SALAD

1 (15½ ounce) can crushed pineapple, undrained

6 (1 ounce) envelopes unflavored gelatin

2 cups buttermilk

1 (16 ounce) container frozen whipped topping

½ cup chopped pecans

In a medium saucepan, heat pineapple and juice. Add gelatin, dissolve and bring to a boil. Remove from heat. Let cool. When the mixture begins to set, fold in buttermilk, whipped topping, and pecans. Chill until ready to serve. Makes 6 servings.

PINEAPPLE FLUFF

Super-Fast

1 (4 serving) box lime flavored gelatin

1 (6 ounce) carton cottage cheese

1 (8 ounce) can crushed pineapple, drained

1 (8 ounce) carton frozen whipped topping

In a large bowl, sprinkle gelatin over cottage cheese. Mix well. Add pineapple and whipped topping. Mix well. Chill until ready to serve. Makes 6 servings.

OLD FASHIONED PINEAPPLE CHEESE SALAD

½ cup sugar

1 cup crushed pineapple, and juice

1 (4 serving) box orange flavored gelatin

1 cup cold water

1 (16 ounce) carton frozen whipped topping

½ cup shredded Cheddar cheese

In a medium saucepan, combine sugar, pineapple, and juice, and bring to a boil. Add gelatin, stirring until dissolved. Add cold water. Let mixture set until partially firm. Add frozen whipped topping and cheese. Place in mold. Chill until firm. May add nuts to mixture before refrigerating. Makes 4 to 6 servings.

RASPBERRY FRUIT SALAD

2 (4 serving) boxes raspberry flavored gelatin

1 (11 ounce) can mandarin oranges

1 (13 ounce) can fruit cocktail

2 medium bananas, sliced thin

1 large apple, diced

½ cup chopped pecans

Prepare gelatin according to package directions. Chill until it just starts to thicken. Drain oranges and fruit cocktail. Add to gelatin. Add bananas, apple, and pecans. Pour into serving dish. Chill until firm. Makes 8 servings.

CREAMY STRAWBERRY SALAD

Super-Fast

1 (4 serving) box strawberry flavored gelatin

½ pint strawberry or vanilla ice cream

1 cup strawberries

In a small saucepan, prepare gelatin according to package directions. In a medium bowl, combine gelatin, ice cream, and strawberries. Mix well, but gently. Chill until firm. Makes 4 servings.

• •

WATERGATE SALAD

1 (4 serving) box instant pistachio pudding

1 (16 ounce) carton frozen whipped topping

2 (8 ounce) cans crushed pineapple, drained

1 cup miniature marshmallows

½ cup chopped nuts

In a large bowl, fold dry pudding into whipped topping. Add pineapple, marshmallows and nuts. Chill. Makes 6 servings.

ORANGES WILL PEEL EASILY AND CLEANLY IF YOU POUR SCALDING WATER OVER THEM AND LET STAND FOR FIVE MINUTES.

APPLE CRUNCH SALAD

1 large apple, chopped

1 cup sliced grapes

1 celery stick, chopped fine

½ cup chopped walnuts

½ cup Miracle Whip®

1 tablespoon sugar

In a large bowl, combine all ingredients. Chill until ready to serve. Makes 2 cups.

Super-Fast

• •

GOOD AND EASY FRUIT SALAD

1 cup orange juice

½ cup sugar

2 tablespoons cornstarch

3 oranges

4 apples

3 bananas

In a small saucepan, combine orange juice, sugar, and corn-starch. Cook and stir over low heat until sauce thickens. Remove from heat and let mixture cool. Cut fruit into bit sized pieces and place in a large bowl. Pour cooled orange sauce over fruit. Makes 6 to 8 servings.

HODGE PODGE SALAD

1 cup shredded coconut

1 cup sour cream

1 cup crushed pineapple, drained

1 cup miniature marshmallows

1 cup cottage cheese

1 cup chopped walnuts

1 cup fruit cocktail, drained

In a large bowl, combine all ingredients, mixing well. Chill before serving. Makes 6 to 8 servings.

MARSHMALLOW HASH

Super-Fast

½ pint whipping cream

32 miniature marshmallows

1 (16 ounce) can crushed pineapple, drained

½ cup chopped cherries

½ cup chopped pecans

¾ cup shredded coconut

In a large bowl, pour whipping cream over marshmallows. Cover and place in refrigerator overnight. The next morning, whip marshmallows, and cream. Fold in remaining ingredients. Makes 6 to 8 servings.

TO KEEP COTTAGE CHEESE FRESH AFTER IT HAS BEEN OPENED, MIX IN A TABLESPOON OF LEMON JUICE. THE FLAVOR OF THE COTTAGE CHEESE WILL NOT BE ALTERED.

QUICK AS A WINK PINEAPPLE SALAD

Super-Fast

1 (8 ounce) package cream
   cheese, softened

1 (8 ounce) carton frozen
   whipped topping, softened

1 cup chopped pecans

1 (8 ounce) can crushed pineapple, drained

1 (13 ounce) jar marshmallow cream

In a large bowl, combine all ingredients. Chill. Makes 6 to 8 servings.

• •

YOGURT FRUIT SALAD

2 tablespoons honey

1 tablespoon orange juice

1 cup plain yogurt

2 cups shredded carrots

½ cup raisins

1 (16 ounce) carton frozen whipped topping

In a large bowl, combine honey, orange juice, and yogurt. Blend well. Add carrots, raisins, and whipped topping, mixing until carrots and raisins are well coated. Chill until ready to serve. Makes 6 to 8 servings.

5 CUP SUPER SALAD

1 cup pineapple chunks, drained

1 cup mandarin orange sections, drained

1 cup flaked coconut

1 cup miniature marshmallows

1 cup sour cream

Super-Fast

In a large bowl, combine pineapple, oranges, coconut, marshmallows, and sour cream. Chill for 24 hours. Makes 8 to 10 servings.

OUT OF THE PAST POTATO SALAD

4 potatoes, boiled and chopped

4 hard boiled eggs, chopped

1 onion, chopped

3 celery stalks, chopped

1½ cups Miracle Whip®

2 tablespoons sugar

1 tablespoon mustard

In a large bowl, combine all ingredients. Mix until potatoes are coated. Chill until ready to serve. Makes 6 to 8 servings.

TO KEEP LETTUCE FROM BECOMING BROWN AND DISCOLORED, BREAK THE LEAVES APART, INSTEAD OF CUTTING THEM WITH A KNIFE.

KIDNEY BEAN SALAD

1 (15 ounce) can kidney beans, drained

4 hard boiled eggs, chopped

½ cup chopped onion

¼ cup sweet pickle relish

⅛ teaspoon prepared mustard

1 tablespoon sugar

¾ cup Miracle Whip®

In a large bowl, combine beans, eggs, onion, and relish. Set aside. In a smaller bowl, combine mustard, sugar, and Miracle Whip®. Pour over bean mixture and mix well. Chill before serving. Makes 6 servings.

• •

BEANS WITH POTATOES SALAD

4 small red potatoes, cut into 1-inch pieces

1 (15 ounce) can three-bean salad, undrained

½ cucumber, seeded and chopped

¼ cup chopped red onion

¼ teaspoon salt

Place potatoes in medium saucepan, add enough water to cover and bring to a boil. Cook 10 to 15 minutes or until tender. Drain and place in a medium bowl, add remaining ingredients. Mix well and let stand at room temperature for 30 minutes before serving. Makes 6 to 8 servings.

CORNBREAD SALAD

2 (8½ ounce) packages cornbread mix

1 cup chopped green pepper

1 cup chopped celery

1 cup chopped onion

1 cup chopped tomatoes

1 pound bacon, cooked and crumbled

Prepare cornbread according to package directions. Cool and crumble into bite sized pieces. In a large bowl, combine crumbled cornbread, green pepper, celery, onion, tomatoes, and bacon. Mix well. Pour cornbread dressing over salad. Makes 6 to 8 servings.

Cornbread Dressing for Salad

⅔ cup sweet pickle juice

¼ cup dill pickle juice

¾ cup mayonnaise

Combine all ingredients in medium bowl. Pour over cornbread salad.

TO KEEP YOUR SALAD TOMATOES FIRM, AND AVOID A WATERY DRESSING, SLICE TOMATOES VERTICALLY INSTEAD OF HORIZONTALLY.

CHICKEN MACARONI SALAD

1 cup chopped cooked chicken

1 (8 ounce) package macaroni, cooked according to package directions

2 stalks celery, chopped

2 green onions, chopped

¾ cup Miracle Whip®

Super-Fast

In a large bowl, combine all ingredients until completely coated. Chill before serving. Makes 4 servings.

• •

HAM MACARONI SALAD

1 (8 ounce) package macaroni

1 teaspoon sugar

3 tablespoons milk

1 cup chopped ham

1 cup Miracle Whip®

1 cup chopped onion

1 cup grated Cheddar cheese

Prepare macaroni according to package directions. Drain and cool. In a large bowl, whisk sugar and milk until mixture is smooth. Add macaroni, ham, Miracle Whip®, onion, and cheese. Chill. Makes 4 servings.

CHICKEN SALAD FOR LUNCH

3 cups chopped cooked chicken

1 cup chopped celery

½ cup chopped green pepper

2 teaspoons diced onion

2 cups seedless grapes

⅔ cups Miracle Whip®

¼ cup half and half

1 teaspoon sugar

In a large bowl, combine all ingredients until chicken is coated. Chill before serving. Makes 4 to 6 servings.

• •

FRESH SPINACH SALAD

1 pound fresh spinach

2 small red onions

3 hard boiled eggs, chopped

6 slices bacon, cooked and crumbled

Remove stems from spinach; wash leaves in lukewarm water and pat dry. Tear spinach into bite sized pieces and place in large bowl. Add onion, eggs, and bacon. Mix well. Serve with your favorite dressing. Makes 6 servings.

USE A PEPPER MILL TO GRIND CARDAMOM AND OTHER SEEDS AND SPICES FOR RECIPES.

WILTED SPINACH SALAD

4 slices bacon, diced

¼ cup white vinegar

4 teaspoons sugar

¼ teaspoon salt

1 (10 ounce) package fresh spinach, washed

5 green onions, chopped with tops

Super-Fast

In a large skillet, cook bacon until crisp. Stir in vinegar, sugar, and salt. Cook over low heat until sugar dissolves. Remove from heat. Add spinach and onions. Toss 1 minute or until spinach wilts. Makes 4 servings.

• •

SLICED CUCUMBER SALAD

1 cucumber

2 cups water

2 tablespoons salt

½ cup sour cream

1 green onion, chopped

3 tablespoons sugar

1 tablespoon vinegar

Score cucumber (run fork tines lengthwise down cucumber), slice and soak in water with 1 tablespoon salt for 3 hours. Drain. Place cucumbers in medium bowl and add 1 tablespoon salt, sour cream, onion, sugar, and vinegar. Mix well. Chill before serving. Makes 2 servings.

FRUIT SALAD FOR LUNCH

1 medium apple, unpeeled, chopped

3 medium oranges, peeled, diced

½ cup sliced grapes

¼ cup raisins

¾ cup Miracle Whip®

1 teaspoon sugar

In medium bowl, combine all ingredients. Mix well. Serve on lettuce cups. Makes 4 servings.

PINEAPPLE HAM SALAD

1 (8 ounce) can pineapple, drained

1 cup diced cooked ham

¼ cup diced Swiss cheese

1 cup grapes, cut in half

1½ cups cream-style cottage cheese

4 cups torn lettuce

In medium bowl, combine all ingredients, except lettuce. Place lettuce on 4 plates; add mixture to each plate. Makes 4 servings.

MARINATED SLICED TOMATOES

4 large tomatoes

¼ cup oil

1 tablespoon lemon juice

½ teaspoon minced garlic

½ teaspoon salt

½ teaspoon oregano

Peel and slice tomatoes. Set aside. Combine oil, lemon juice, garlic, salt, and oregano. Pour over tomatoes. Cover and chill before serving. Makes 6 to 8 servings.

• •

PINEAPPLE CABBAGE SLAW

3 cups grated cabbage

½ teaspoon salt

½ cup Italian dressing

½ cup sugar

¾ cup crushed pineapple

3 tablespoons vinegar

1 small carrot, grated

In a large bowl, toss all ingredients until cabbage is coated. Chill before serving. Makes 6 servings.

TO TEST YOUR KITCHEN SCALE, PLACE NINE PENNIES ON IT. THEY SHOULD WEIGH ONE OUNCE.

SWEET-SOUR COLE SLAW

⅔ cup sugar

1 teaspoon salt

⅓ cup cider vinegar

1 cup whipping cream (do not whip)

1½ pounds shredded cabbage

In a medium bowl, combine sugar, salt, vinegar, and whipping cream. Pour over shredded cabbage. Chill at least 4 hours before serving. Makes 6 to 8 servings.

• •

DELICIOUS POPPY SEED DRESSING

½ cup honey

½ teaspoon salt

⅓ cup wine vinegar

1 cup salad oil

1 tablespoon poppy seeds

In a small bowl, combine honey, salt, and vinegar. Gradually add oil, stirring constantly. Add poppy seeds. Pour into covered container and refrigerate. Shake before serving. Makes 2 cups.

RUSSIAN DRESSING

1 cup vegetable oil

½ cup ketchup

⅓ cup vinegar

2 tablespoons sugar

1 teaspoon salt

½ teaspoon grated onion

In a medium bowl, combine all ingredients, mixing thoroughly. Makes 1¾ cups.

• •

THREE STEP LETTUCE DRESSING

1 cup Miracle Whip®

⅓ cup milk

1 tablespoon sugar

Super-Fast

In a small bowl, combine all ingredients and pour over lettuce salad. Makes 1⅓ cups.

• •

OVERNIGHT DRESSING

1 cup mayonnaise

¼ cup sugar

2 tablespoons vinegar

In a small bowl, combine all ingredients. Refrigerate overnight. Use over lettuce or as a dip for fresh vegetables. Makes 1 cup.

THOUSAND ISLAND DRESSING

1 cup Miracle Whip®

½ cup ketchup

2 tablespoons sweet relish

1 hard boiled egg, finely chopped

In a small bowl, combine all ingredients. Chill before serving. Makes 1½ cups.

● ●

FRENCH DRESSING

1 (10¾ ounce) can tomato soup

1 cup salad oil

¼ cup sugar

½ cup vinegar

⅛ teaspoon garlic salt

In a small bowl, combine all ingredients. Pour into a jar, cover, and chill. Shake before serving. Makes 3 servings.

CLEAN YOUR MICROWAVE BY PLACING A WET PAPER TOWEL IN THE OVEN AND MICROWAVE ON HIGH FOR 4 MINUTES. WHEN THE PAPER TOWEL COOLS A BIT, USE IT TO WIPE THE OVEN CLEAN.

CHUNKY VEGETABLE SOUP

Super-Fast

2 cups cooked ham

¾ teaspoon dried thyme

¼ teaspoon pepper

1 (16 ounce) package frozen green beans, potatoes, onions, and red peppers

2 (14½ ounce) cans ready to serve chicken broth

In a 2 quart saucepan, combine all ingredients. Heat to boiling. Reduce heat and simmer uncovered 8 minutes or until vegetables are tender. Makes 6 servings.

Per Serving: Calories-125, Protein-14 gm, Fat-5 gm, Carbohydrates-7 gm, Cholesterol-25 mg, Sodium-1300 mg.

• •

TORTELLINI SOUP

4 cups water

1 (1.4 ounce) package vegetable soup and recipe mix

1 (9 ounce) package cheese-filled tortellini

1 (10 ounce) package frozen spinach, thawed and drained

Parmesan cheese

In a 3 quart saucepan, combine water and soup mix. Heat to boiling, stirring often. Reduce heat to low. Add tortellini and spinach. Simmer uncovered until tortellini is tender. Sprinkle each serving with grated Parmesan cheese. Makes 6 servings.

Per Serving: Calories-105, Protein-7 gm , Fat-3 gm, Carbohydrates-15 gm, Cholesterol-40 mg, Sodium-710 mg.

TASTY CORN CHOWDER

Super-Fast

½ cup chopped cooked ham

1½ cups skim milk

1 (16 ounce) package frozen corn

1 (10¾ ounce) can cream of celery soup

2 green onions, chopped with tops

In a 3 quart saucepan, combine all ingredients. Heat to boiling, stirring occasionally. Reduce heat to low. Simmer uncovered for 10 minutes. Makes 4 servings.

Per Serving: Calories-215, Protein-11 gm , Fat-6 gm, Carbohydrates-32 gm, Cholesterol-15 mg, Sodium-860 mg.

NEW ENGLAND CLAM CHOWDER

2 slices bacon, cut into ½ inch pieces

2 green onions, sliced

*2 (16 ounce) cans minced clams, drained and
    liquid reserved*

2 potatoes, diced

2 cups skim milk

In a 2 quart saucepan, combine bacon and onion. Cook until bacon is crisp. Add enough water to reserved clam juice to measure 1 cup. Add clam liquid, clams, and potatoes to bacon mixture. Heat to boiling, reduce heat to medium. Cover and cook for 15 minutes. Stir in milk. Heat until hot. Makes 4 servings.

Per Serving: Calories-185, Protein-17 gm , Fat-3 gm, Carbohydrates-25 gm, Cholesterol-35 mg, Sodium-170mg.

SIRLOIN STEAK SALAD

2 teaspoons vegetable oil

¾ pound lean sirloin, cut into 2 inch strips

2 green peppers, cut into strips

1 small onion, thinly sliced

4 cups (bite sized pieces) salad greens

⅓ cup fat free Italian dressing

¼ cup plain fat free yogurt

In a medium skillet, heat oil until hot. Add steak and brown. Remove from skillet. Add peppers and onions to oil, stir and cook until crisp-tender. Add beef. Place salad greens on a serving platter. Top with beef mixture. Pour dressing over beef. Top with yogurt.

Per Serving: Calories-150, Protein-19 gm, Fat-5 gm, Carbohydrates-8 gm, Cholesterol-45 mg, Sodium-240 mg.

ROBUST CHICKEN SALAD

2 cups chopped cooked chicken

4 cups broccoli, chopped

1 (16 ounce) package slaw mix

2 small red apples, chopped

½ cup light mayonnaise

2 tablespoons cider vinegar

In a large bowl toss together chicken, broccoli, slaw mix and apples. In a small bowl combine mayonnaise and vinegar, mix well, pour over salad and toss lightly to coat. Makes 4 servings.

Per Serving: Calories-327 gm, Carbohydrate-18 gm, Cholesterol-70 mg, Sodium-360 mg.

LOBSTER SALAD

1 (10 ounce) package salad greens

1 (8 ounce) package imitation lobster chunks

1 (11 ounce) can mandarin oranges, chilled and drained

1 small cucumber, sliced into ¼ inch pieces

⅓ cup fat free Ranch dressing

In a large bowl, toss all ingredients until coated. Makes 4 servings.

Per Serving: Calories-120, Protein-13 gm , Fat-1 gram, Carbohydrates-17 gm, Cholesterol-40 mg, Sodium-480 mg.

TOSSED TUNA SALAD

1 (10 ounce) can water-packed tuna, drained

¾ cup chopped celery

1 (8 ounce) can peas, drained

½ cup fat-free mayonnaise

In a medium bowl, toss all ingredients until coated. Chill before serving. Serve on a bed of lettuce. Makes 4 servings.

Per Serving: Calories-160, Protein-22 gm, Fat-2 gm, Carbohydrates-12 gm, Cholesterol-30 mg, Sodium-680 mg.

TO MAKE A FUNNEL FOR FILLING SALT AND PEPPER SHAKERS, USE A CLEAN ENVELOPE WITH THE CORNER CUT OFF.

BOW-TIE PASTA SALAD

1 cup cooked bow-tie pasta

1 tomato, diced

¼ cup diced celery

¼ cup diced green onion

¼ cup thinly sliced scallions

1 tablespoon red wine vinegar

1 tablespoon salad oil

⅛ teaspoon salt

¼ teaspoon pepper

In a large bowl, combine all ingredients. Mix well. Cover and chill before serving. Makes 2 servings.

Per Serving: Calories-158, Protein-4 gm, Fat-5 gm, Carbohydrates-24 gm, Cholesterol-25 mg, Sodium-205 mg.

ITALIAN PASTA SALAD

1 cup cooked pasta nuggets

1 cup carrot strips

1 cup fresh broccoli florets

1 cup sliced mushrooms

½ cup Italian salad dressing

In a medium bowl, combine all ingredients, mix well. Cover, chill one hour to blend flavors. Makes 10-½ cup servings.

Per Serving: Calories-100, Protein-2 gm, Total fat-6 gm, Carbohydrates-10 gm, Cholesterol-0 mg, Sodium-100 mg.

ORANGE CARROT SALAD

1 pound carrots, peeled and grated

1 cup fresh orange juice

¼ cup golden raisins

1 tablespoon minced ginger

1 teaspoon salt

¼ teaspoon red pepper

In a large bowl, combine all ingredients, tossing to coat. Cover and refrigerate 1 hour before serving. Makes 8 servings.

Per Serving: Calories-140, Protein-2 gm , Fat-7 gm, Carbohydrates-20 gm, Cholesterol-0 mg, Sodium-290 mg.

TANGY COLESLAW

Super-Fast

1 (8 ounce) can crushed unsweetened pineapple, with juice

3 tablespoons chili sauce

½ teaspoon salt

⅛ teaspoon pepper

1 (16 ounce) package shredded cabbage

In a large bowl, combine pineapple with juice, chili sauce, salt, and pepper. Mix well. Add cabbage and toss to coat. Chill before serving. Makes 4 servings.

Per Serving: Calories-75, Protein-2 gm, Fat-0 gm, Carbohydrates-18 gm, Cholesterol-0 mg, Sodium-460 mg.

MAKE-AHEAD COLESLAW

1 (16 ounce package coleslaw mix)

½ cup chopped red onions

1 (2 ¼ ounce) can sliced olives, drained

1 cup creamy Caesar salad dressing

1 cup croutons

In a large bowl combine coleslaw, onions and olives. Add salad dressing and toss to coat. Just before serving, top with croutons. 14-½ cup servings.

Per Serving: Calories-100, Protein-1 gm, Total fat-8 gm, Carbohydrates-5 gm, Cholesterol-3 mg, Sodium-270 mg.

• •

GARLIC SALAD DRESSING

4 cups low-fat yogurt

2 cucumbers, peeled, seeded, and diced

2 garlic gloves, minced

3 tablespoons finely chopped fresh dill

In a medium bowl, whisk all ingredients until smooth. Cover and chill. Makes 4 cups.

Per Serving (1 tablespoon): Calories-9, Protein-1 gram, Fat-trace, Carbohydrates-1 gm, Cholesterol-1 mg, Sodium-10 mg.

FRUIT SALAD DRESSING

½ cup low-fat vanilla yogurt

½ cup mashed banana

¾ cup diced kiwi

2 tablespoons frozen pineapple juice
   concentrate

½ teaspoon coconut extract

Place all ingredients in a blender. Cover and blend until smooth. Makes 1½ cups.

Per Serving: Calories-49, Protein-1.2 gm, Fat-0.2 gm, Carbohydrates-11.4 gm, Cholesterol-.04 mg, Sodium-12.7 mg.

• •

VEGGIE DIP OR SALAD DRESSING

¼ cup crumbled blue cheese

½ cup non-fat plain yogurt

½ cover garlic, minced

½ teaspoon Dijon mustard

In a small bowl, cream blue cheese. Add yogurt, garlic, and mustard. Mix well. Makes 6 servings.

Per Serving: Calories-31, Protein-2 gm, Fat-2 gm, Carbohydrates-2 gm, Cholesterol-5 mg, Sodium-98 mg.

Putting on the Ritz

(Beef, Pork, Poultry, and Seafood)

CROCKPOT ROAST

3 potatoes, sliced

3 carrots, sliced

1 onion, sliced

Salt and pepper to taste

3 pound beef roast

½ cup beef broth

Place vegetables in bottom of crockpot. Salt and pepper beef to taste. Place roast on top of vegetables. Add broth. Cover. Cook on low for 10 to 12 hours (high for 5 to 6 hours). Makes 4 to 6 servings.

• •

END OF THE DAY ROAST

2 pounds boneless beef chuck

4 potatoes, peeled and quartered

3 carrots, sliced

1 (1 ounce) dry onion soup mix

1 (14 ounce) can stewed tomatoes

In crock pot, combine all ingredients. Cover. Cook on low 8 to 10 hours. Makes 4 servings.

A LITTLE BIT DIFFERENT ROAST

2½ or 3 pound chuck roast
Vegetable oil
1 (1 ounce) packet dried onion soup mix
1 (10¾ ounce) can cream of mushroom soup
2 teaspoons Worcestershire sauce
2 teaspoons A-1® steak sauce

Preheat oven to 350 °. In a large skillet, brown roast in a small amount of oil. Place in roasting pan. In a small bowl, combine soups, Worcestershire sauce, and A-1® sauce, mixing well. Pour mixture over roast. Cover. Bake at 350° for 2½ to 3 hours. Makes 6 servings.

MEXIE MACK BURGERS

Super-Fast

1½ pounds ground beef
1 (1.5 ounce) packet taco seasoning
¼ cup ketchup
¼ teaspoon garlic salt
1 small onion, chopped
Salsa
Grated Cheddar cheese

In a medium bowl, combine ground beef, taco seasoning, ketchup, garlic salt, and onion. Shape into patties. Grill or broil. Top with salsa and grated cheese. Makes 6 to 8 servings.

ITALIAN STYLE HAMBURGERS

1 pound ground beef

1 egg, beaten

¼ cup chopped onion

½ cup Italian style bread crumbs

In a large bowl, combine all ingredients. Form into 6 patties. Grill or fry. Makes 6 servings.

• •

HAMBURGER MEAT CUPS

1 pound ground beef

½ tablespoon onion flakes

1 teaspoon salt

1 (10 count) tube refrigerated biscuits

1 cup grated cheese

Preheat oven to 375°. Spray muffin tins with vegetable cooking spray. In a medium skillet, brown ground beef. Drain on paper towels. Return to skillet and combine with onion flakes and salt. Place a biscuit in the bottom of each muffin cup. Add beef and top with cheese. Bake at 375° for 10 minutes. Makes 6 to 8 servings.

TO KEEP BACON FROM SHRINKING AND CURLING DURING FRYING, SOAK THE SLICES IN COLD WATER FOR A FEW MINUTES BEFORE PLACING THEM IN A COLD SKILLET. TURN THE BACON OFTEN AND DRAIN THE FAT DURING COOKING.

MEAT LOAF WITH A TWIST

2 pounds ground beef

1 onion, chopped

2 eggs

1 cup cracker crumbs

½ cup milk

½ cup grated Cheddar cheese

2 teaspoons garlic salt

1 (10¾ ounce) can tomato soup

Preheat oven to 350°. Lightly grease a 9 x 5 x 3 inch loaf
pan. Set aside. In a large bowl, combine ground beef, onion,
eggs, crumbs, milk, cheese, and garlic salt. Form into loaf
and place in prepared pan. Bake at 350° for 30 minutes.
Pour soup over meat loaf. Bake an additional 30 minutes.
Makes 6 servings.

COUNTRY MEAT LOAF

1 egg

1½ pounds ground beef

½ cup chopped onion

½ cup diced celery

1¾ cups ketchup

1 cup cracker crumbs

Preheat oven to 350°. In a large bowl, slightly beat egg.
Add ground beef, onion, celery, ¾ cup of the ketchup, and
cracker crumbs. Mix well. Shape into loaf. Place on rack
in bottom of shallow pan, cover with 1 cup of the ketchup.
Top with foil. Bake at 350° for 1½ hours. Makes 6 to 8
servings.

GREAT TASTING ROUND STEAK

⅓ cup honey

⅓ cup lime juice

2 tablespoons vegetable oil

2 tablespoons prepared mustard

2 cloves garlic, minced

Salt and pepper to taste

2 pound round steak

In a small bowl, combine honey, lime juice, oil, mustard, garlic, salt, and pepper. Mix well. Pour mixture over steak. Refrigerate 6 to 8 hours. Grill to desired doneness. Thinly slice on the diagonal. Makes 6 servings.

• •

THE BEST OVEN BAKED STEAK

3 pound round steak

1 teaspoon salt

1 teaspoon pepper

1 cup flour

Vegetable oil

1½ cups cream of mushroom soup

1¼ cups milk

Preheat oven to 350°. Cut steak into serving size pieces. In a small bowl, combine salt, pepper, and flour. Dredge steak pieces in flour. In a large skillet, heat oil. Place steak pieces into oil to brown. Place meat in 2 quart baking dish. Combine soup and milk and pour over meat. Cover. Bake at 350° for 1½ to 2 hours. Makes 6 servings.

SUPER TASTY CLUB STEAKS

2 tablespoons butter

1 garlic pod

4 club steaks, 1 inch thick

Pepper

Salt

Super-Fast

In a large skillet, melt butter. Add garlic pod. Sprinkle steaks with pepper. Cook over low heat for 5 to 6 minutes. Salt meat before serving. Makes 4 servings.

● ●

TASTY T-BONE STEAKS

4 T-bone steaks

Salt and pepper to taste

1½ teaspoons minced garlic

½ cup butter, melted

In a 15 x 10 x 1 inch pan, marinate steaks for one hour in salt, pepper, garlic, and butter. Grill or broil. Makes 4 servings.

TENDERIZE STEAKS FOR BROILING BY SOAKING THEM IN MILK FOR ONE HOUR BEFORE COOKING.

OLD SOUTH CHICKEN FRIED STEAK

1 egg, beaten

¼ cup milk

½ teaspoon salt

1 teaspoon pepper

1½ pound round steak, tenderized

1 cup flour

⅓ cup vegetable oil

In a shallow pan, combine egg, milk, salt, and pepper. Pour flour into another shallow pan. Cut steak into serving size pieces. Dip each piece into egg mixture, then into flour. In a large skillet, heat oil and brown steak on both sides. Lower heat and fry until done. Makes 4 servings.

● ●

BAKED SWISS STEAK

2 tablespoons flour

¾ tablespoon salt

½ tablespoon pepper

1½ pound round steak

3 tablespoons vegetable oil

1½ cups canned stewed tomatoes

1 onion, sliced

Preheat oven to 325°. In a shallow pan, combine flour, salt, and pepper. Set aside. Cut steak into serving size pieces. Dredge meat in flour mixture. In a large skillet, heat oil and brown steak on both sides. Place steak in 13 x 9 inch baking dish. Top with tomatoes and onions. Bake at 325° for 2 hours. Makes 4 servings.

CROCKPOT SWISS STEAK

1½ pound round steak

2 tablespoons flour

Salt and pepper to taste

1 onion, sliced

1 carrot, chopped

1 rib celery, chopped

1 (15 ounce) can tomato sauce

Cut steak into serving size pieces. In a shallow pan, combine flour, salt, and pepper. Dredge meat in flour. Place onion in the bottom of a crockpot. Add meat and vegetables. Pour tomato sauce over mixture. Cover and cook on low for 8 to 10 hours. Makes 4 to 6 servings.

• •

QUICK FIX BRISKET

3 pound brisket

1 (16 ounce) bottle Italian dressing

In a shallow baking pan, marinate brisket in Italian dressing, 8 hours or overnight. Preheat oven to 325°. Cover pan with foil and bake at 325° for 3 or 4 hours. Makes 6 to 8 servings.

TO KEEP HAMBURGERS FROM COMING APART DURING COOKING, MIX IN A SMALL AMOUNT OF FLOUR BEFORE COOKING.

BARBECUED BRISKET

1 (1 ounce) packet dry onion soup mix

2 cups barbecue sauce

1 tablespoon sugar

1 tablespoon maple syrup

3 to 4 pound brisket

Preheat oven to 250 °. In a small bowl, combine soup mix, barbecue sauce, sugar, and syrup. Place brisket in a shallow baking pan and cover with sauce. Cover pan with foil, sealing edges, and bake at 250° for 8 hours. Makes 8 to 10 servings.

• •

BARBECUED SPARERIBS

½ cup ketchup

1 teaspoon Worcestershire sauce

1 tablespoon sugar

¼ cup packed brown sugar

1½ cups barbecue sauce

1 side of spareribs

2 onions, sliced

Preheat oven to 250°. In a medium bowl, combine ketchup, Worcestershire sauce, sugars, and barbecue sauce, mixing well. Cut spareribs into serving size pieces. In a large roasting pan, layer spareribs and onions, and cover with sauce. Cover pan with foil, sealing edges. Bake at 250° for 1½ hours. Uncover and bake an additional 30 minutes. Makes 4 servings.

OVEN BARBECUED PORK RIBS

6 pounds pork spareribs

3 cups ketchup

1½ cups packed brown sugar

¾ cup chopped onions

1 teaspoon garlic powder

4 teaspoons liquid smoke seasoning

Preheat oven to 350°. Cut ribs into serving size pieces. Place ribs in a shallow baking pan and bake uncovered at 350° for 30 minutes. In a medium saucepan, combine ketchup, brown sugar, onions, garlic powder, and liquid smoke. Simmer for 20 minutes, stirring frequently. Drain ribs and coat with sauce. Cover pan with foil, sealing edges. Bake for 35 minutes. Uncover and bake an additional 5 minutes, basting ribs with sauce. Makes 6 to 8 servings.

● ●

NO PEEK BARBECUE RIBS

2½ to 3 pounds spareribs

Salt and pepper to taste

1 teaspoon sugar

1 (16 ounce) bottle smoky flavored barbecue sauce

1 large onion, sliced

Preheat broiler. Sprinkle ribs with salt and pepper. Broil for 15 minutes, turning once, to brown. Add sugar to barbecue sauce and set aside. Slice ribs into serving size pieces. Using a crockpot, layer onions and ribs, covering with sauce. Cover and cook on low for 8 to 10 hours (high for 4 to 5 hours). Makes 4 to 6 servings.

BARBECUED PORK RIBS

1½ cups barbecue sauce

1 tablespoon sugar

1 tablespoon maple syrup

3 pounds pork ribs

Preheat over to 300°. In a medium bowl, combine barbecue sauce, sugar, and syrup. Place ribs in a shallow baking pan. Coat ribs on both sides with sauce. Marinate for 1 hour. Bake uncovered at 300° for 2 hours or until ribs are cooked through. Makes 4 servings.

BREADED PORK CHOPS

Super-Fast

2 eggs, beaten

¼ cup milk

1 teaspoon salt

4 pork chops, sliced ½ inch thick

1½ cups cracker crumbs

⅓ cup vegetable oil

⅓ cup water

In a medium bowl, combine eggs, milk, and salt. Dip chops in egg mixture and then coat with cracker crumbs. Heat oil in medium skillet. Place chops in oil and brown on both sides. Add water. Reduce heat, cover and cook until done.

POUR MEAT BROTH THROUGH A COFFEE FILTER TO STRAIN OUT THE FAT.

CRANBERRY PORK CHOPS

4 thick pork chops

½ cup bread crumbs

½ cup cranberry chutney

1 tablespoon dried rosemary

Preheat oven to 350°. Cut a pocket in the side of each pork chop and place chops in shallow baking pan. In a small bowl, combine crumbs and chutney. Stuff chops with chutney mixture. Sprinkle rosemary over chops. Bake uncovered at 350° for 45 minutes. Makes 4 servings.

● ●

PORK TENDERLOIN ON THE GRILL

2 tablespoons coarse salt

2 tablespoons garlic powder

¼ cup packed brown sugar

1 teaspoon celery salt

4 pound pork tenderloin

In a small bowl, combine salt, garlic, sugar, and celery salt. Rub mixture into meat. Grill to desired doneness. Makes 8 servings.

LICKIN' GOOD PORK CHOPS

½ cup flour

1 tablespoon salt

1½ teaspoons dry mustard

½ teaspoon garlic powder

6 to 8 lean pork chops

2 tablespoons vegetable oil

1 (10¾ ounce) can chicken and rice soup

In a medium bowl, combine flour, salt, mustard, and garlic powder. Dredge pork chops in mixture. In a large skillet, brown chops on both sides in oil. Place chops in crockpot. Add soup. Cover and cook on low 6 to 8 hours. Makes 6 to 8 servings.

FRUITED PORK CHOPS

Super-Fast

4 pork chops

Vegetable oil

1 (8.25 ounce) can pineapple chunks, drained

½ cup dried apricots

½ cup sweet and spicy French salad dressing

In a medium skillet, brown pork chops in hot oil. Drain off fat. Place pineapple and apricots on top of pork chops. Pour dressing over fruit. Cover and simmer until pork chops are done. Makes 4 servings.

PORK CHOPS ITALIANO

4 to 5 pork chops

Vegetable oil or non-stick cooking spray

1 (10¾ ounce) can tomato soup

1 (4 ounce) can green chiles

1 cup grated mozzarella cheese

In a large skillet, brown pork chops in oil. Pour soup and chiles over pork chops. Cover and cook over low heat for 45 minutes. Sprinkle cheese over chops, cover and cook for an additional 5 minutes. Makes 4 to 5 servings.

• •

PAN FRIED PORK CHOPS

1 teaspoon salt

1 teaspoon pepper

4 pork chops

1 cup flour

⅓ cup vegetable oil

Salt and pepper pork chops. Dredge chops in flour. In a large skillet, brown chops in hot oil, turning once. Reduce heat and fry chops until done. Makes 4 servings.

FOR READY-TO-EAT BACON, COOK THE ENTIRE PACKAGE, DRAIN IT, PLACE IT IN PLASTIC FREEZER BAGS, AND FREEZE. REMOVE THE SLICES YOU NEED AND REHEAT IN THE MICROWAVE.

BAKED HAM SLICE

1½ pounds fully cooked ham slice

¾ cup packed brown sugar

½ cup pineapple juice

1 teaspoon mustard

1 tablespoon maple syrup

Preheat oven to 350°. Place ham slice in medium baking pan. In a small bowl, combine brown sugar, juice, mustard, and syrup. Mix well. Spread mixture over ham. Cover and bake for 60 minutes. Makes 4 servings.

• •

HAM WITH PINEAPPLE SAUCE

1 (4 to 6 pound) fully cooked, boneless ham

½ cup diced onions

¼ cup margarine

1 cup ketchup

1 cup pineapple preserves

Preheat oven to 325°. Using a shallow baking pan with a rack, bake ham at 325° for 2 hours. In a small saucepan, combine onion, margarine, ketchup, and preserves. Cook and stir until onions are tender. During last 10 minutes of baking, baste ham with sauce. Serve with remaining sauce. Makes 16 to 20 servings.

CROCKPOT BAKED HAM

½ cup water

½ cup packed brown sugar

¾ cup pineapple juice

3 to 4 pound precooked ham

Pour water into crockpot. In a small bowl, mix brown sugar and juice. Place ham on a large piece of aluminum foil. Pour juice mixture over ham and close foil into a tight package. Place ham in crockpot. Cook on high for 1½ hours. Makes 6-8 servings.

• •

FRIED COUNTRY HAM

Super-Fast

4 slices country ham

1½ cups milk

⅓ cup vegetable oil

In a shallow pan, soak ham in milk for 30 minutes. Rinse in water. This will take out some of the salt. Cut ham into small slices. In a medium skillet, fry ham in oil until brown on both sides. Makes 4 to 6 servings. This is great served over biscuits.

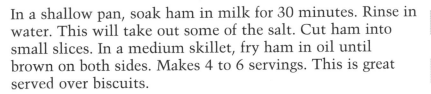

EASILY REMOVE CANNED HAM FROM ITS CONTAINER BY RUNNING HOT TAP WATER OVER THE CAN FOR A FEW MINUTES BEFORE OPENING.

MOZZARELLA BAKED CHICKEN

4 chicken breasts, skinless and boneless

Salt

Pepper

8 ounces sliced mozzarella cheese

1 cup sour cream

1 (10¾ ounce) can cream of mushroom soup

Preheat oven to 350°. In a shallow baking dish, place chicken breasts in a single layer and sprinkle with salt and pepper. Place cheese slices on chicken. In a small bowl, combine sour cream and soup. Pour over chicken. Cover and bake at 350° for 1 hour. Makes 4 servings.

• •

BAKED CHICKEN AND RUSSIAN DRESSING

*4 chicken breasts, boneless
    and skinless*

*1 (8 ounce) bottle Russian
    dressing*

Super-Fast

1 (1 ounce) packet dry onion soup mix

½ cup water

Preheat oven to 350°. Place chicken in a shallow baking dish. In a small bowl, combine dressing, soup and water. Pour half of mixture over chicken. Bake uncovered at 350° for 30 minutes. Pour remaining mixture over chicken. Bake an additional 30 minutes. Makes 4 servings.

HONEY BASTED BAKED CHICKEN

½ cup honey

¼ cup Dijon mustard

1 clove garlic, minced

1 small onion, diced

4 chicken breasts, skinless and boneless

2 cups crushed corn flakes

Salt and pepper to taste

Preheat oven to 350°. In a small bowl, combine honey, mustard, garlic, and onion. Dip chicken in mixture and roll in corn flakes. Coat a baking sheet with non-stick cooking spray. Place chicken on baking sheet. Sprinkle with salt and pepper. Bake at 350° for 35 to 40 minutes. Makes 4 servings.

• •

CHEESY CHICKEN BREASTS

½ cup margarine, melted

4 chicken breasts, boneless and skinless

⅓ cup flour

Salt and pepper to taste

1¼ cups evaporated milk

1 (10¾ ounce) can cream of mushroom soup

1½ cups grated cheese

Preheat oven to 350°. Pour melted butter into 11 x 7 inch baking pan. Coat chicken breasts in flour, then salt and pepper to taste. Place chicken in baking pan. Bake uncovered at 350° for 30 minutes. In a small bowl, combine milk, soup, and cheese. Pour mixture over chicken. Return to oven and bake for 15 minutes. Makes 4 servings.

M'M M'M GOOD CHICKEN

Super-Fast

4 chicken halves, boneless and skinless

1 tablespoon vegetable oil

1 (10¾ ounce) can cream of mushroom soup

½ cup water

In a large skillet, brown chicken in oil. In a small bowl, combine soup and water and pour over chicken. Cover and simmer over medium heat for 30 minutes, or until done. Makes 4 to 6 servings.

PERFECT BAKED CHICKEN

3 pound chicken

½ cup margarine, melted

1½ teaspoons salt

¼ cup water

Preheat oven to 350°. Wash chicken and pat dry. Place chicken in 2 quart baking dish. Pour butter over chicken, then sprinkle with salt. Pour water into baking dish. Cover and bake for 1 hour at 350°. Uncover and bake an additional 30 minutes. Makes 6 servings.

TO MAKE PRETTY GRAVY FOR CHICKEN AND NOODLE DISHES, MIX IN A FEW DROPS OF YELLOW FOOD COLORING.

TORTILLA MEXICAN CHICKEN

3 cups broken tortilla chips

2 cups shredded, cooked chicken

1 (10¾ ounce) can cream of chicken soup

1 (4 ounce) can green chiles

1 cup chopped onion

1 cup grated Cheddar cheese

Preheat oven to 350°. In a 13 x 9 inch baking pan, layer chips and chicken, spreading evenly. In a small bowl, combine soup, chiles, and onion. Pour mixture over chicken. Top with cheese. Bake uncovered at 350° for 35 minutes. Makes 4 to 6 servings.

• •

FIX AND GO CHICKEN

4 boneless, skinless chicken breast halves

1 (15 ounce) can tomato sauce

1 (4 ounce) can sliced mushrooms, drained

½ cup water

½ teaspoon Italian seasoning

In crock pot, place chicken. In medium bowl, combine sauce, mushrooms, water, and Italian seasoning. Pour over chicken. Cover. Cook on high for 3 to 4 hours and low 6 to 8 hours. Serve over rice. Makes 4 servings.

GRILLED TERIYAKI CHICKEN

1 tablespoon soy sauce

1 cup packed brown sugar

1 clove garlic, pressed

½ teaspoon ginger

½ cup white wine

4 chicken breasts, skinless and boneless

In a large bowl, combine soy sauce, brown sugar, garlic, ginger, and wine. Marinate chicken in mixture for 1 hour. Grill, basting with marinade. Makes 4 servings.

• •

TRUE SOUTHERN FRIED CHICKEN

2½ to 3 pound fryer chicken

1½ teaspoons salt

1½ teaspoons pepper

1½ cups flour

½ cup vegetable oil

1 stick margarine

Cut chicken into serving size pieces. Salt and pepper chicken and roll in flour. In a large skillet, heat oil and margarine until hot. Place chicken in hot oil and brown. Cover and cook over low heat for 20 minutes. Uncover and cook 5 additional minutes, turning frequently. Makes 4 to 6 servings.

TO MAKE READY-TO-EAT MARINATED CHICKEN, PLACE MARINADE AND CHICKEN IN FREEZER BAGS. SHAKE BAG TO COAT CHICKEN AND FREEZE UNTIL READY TO COOK.

DIPPING CHICKEN TENDERS

¾ cup plain bread crumbs

3 tablespoons Parmesan cheese

2 eggs, beaten

1½ pounds chicken tenders

1½ cups barbecue sauce

Preheat oven to 375°. Coat a cookie sheet with non-stick cooking spray. In a shallow pan, combine bread crumbs and cheese. Place eggs in a small bowl and dip chicken into egg. Roll chicken in bread crumbs. Place on cookie sheet. Bake at 375 ° for 35 minutes. Serve with barbecue sauce for dipping. Makes 4 servings.

DELICIOUS TURKEY CASSEROLE

2 to 3 pound boneless turkey breast

3 tablespoons butter

5 cups sweet potatoes, peeled and cubed

½ cup sweetened whole cranberries

¾ cup orange juice

Salt

Preheat oven to 350°. Place turkey breast in a medium roasting pan. Rub butter over turkey. Arrange sweet potatoes and cranberries around turkey. Pour orange juice over turkey, then sprinkle with salt. Cover with foil. Bake at 350° for one hour. Uncover and baste turkey with juice. Continue baking until turkey is tender (about 30 minutes). Makes 8-10 servings.

TURKEY MEAT LOAF

2 pounds ground turkey

1 (1 ounce) packet dry onion soup

½ cup plain bread crumbs

4 ounces grated mozzarella cheese

¼ cup ketchup

Preheat oven to 350°. Coat a 9 x 5 inch loaf pan with non-stick cooking spray. In a large bowl, combine turkey, soup mix, and bread crumbs. Form half the mixture into a 9 x 5 inch loaf. Sprinkle grated cheese on top of loaf. Place remaining mixture on top of cheese and seal edges. Place meat loaf in pan. Pour ketchup over meat loaf. Bake at 350° for 45 minutes. Makes 6 servings.

• •

BAKE IN A BAG TURKEY

1 tablespoon flour

1 turkey size oven cooking bag

2 stalks celery, sliced

1 onion, sliced

16-20 pound frozen turkey, thawed

3 tablespoons butter, melted

Preheat oven to 350°. Shake flour in oven bag to coat. Place bag in a large roasting pan. Add vegetables. Brush turkey with butter. Place turkey in bag. Close bag with nylon tie. Cut slits in top. Bake at 350° for 3 ½ hours or until done. Makes 8 to 12 servings.

TO REMOVE THE WILD TASTE FROM GAME MEAT, SOAK THE MEAT IN BAKING SODA AND WATER OVERNIGHT IN THE REFRIGERATOR. RINSE AND PAT DRY BEFORE COOKING.

FRENCH FRIED FISH DISH

1 (16 ounce) package frozen fish fillets

½ teaspoon salt

½ cup tartar sauce

1 (3 ounce) can French fried onions

Preheat oven to 350°. Cut fish into 5 serving pieces. Layer fish in an 8 x 8 x 2 inch baking dish. Sprinkle fish with salt. Bake at 350° for 30 minutes. Remove from oven, spread tartar sauce over fish. Top with onions. Return to oven and bake until onions are crisp. Makes 5 servings.

• •

FISH AND VEGETABLES IN FOIL

1 (16 ounce) package frozen block fish fillets

1 tablespoon lemon juice

½ teaspoon onion salt

1 cup chopped green pepper

1 cup chopped tomato

2 tablespoons butter

Let fish thaw for 30 minutes. Preheat oven to 450°. Cut fish into four pieces. Place each piece on a 12 inch square of aluminum foil. Sprinkle fish with lemon juice and onion salt. Add green pepper and tomatoes. Put a pat of butter on each fish fillet. Close foil around fish. Place in a shallow baking pan. Bake at 450° for 45 minutes. Makes 4 servings.

CAMPFIRE FISH

⅓ cup flour

½ teaspoon salt

⅛ teaspoon pepper

4 (12 ounces each) whole trout

½ cup margarine

In a shallow pan, combine flour, salt, and pepper. Dredge fish in flour. Place fish in a well-greased wire grill basket. Grill over open fire until fish is flaky. Baste often with margarine. Makes 4 servings.

• •

SOUTHERN FRIED CATFISH

½ cup flour

½ cup cornmeal

1 teaspoon salt

1 teaspoon pepper

2 eggs

½ cup milk

4 catfish fillets

½ cup vegetable oil

1 tablespoon butter

In a shallow pan, combine flour, cornmeal, salt, and pepper. In a small bowl, combine eggs and milk Dip fish in egg mixture, then in dry mixture. Set aside in a medium skillet, heat oil and butter and fry fish until tender. Turn once. Makes 2 or 4 servings.

OVEN FRIED TROUT

1⅓ *cups sour cream*

1 tablespoon lemon juice

1 tablespoon chili powder

1 pound trout fillets

¾ *cup finely crushed corn chips*

2 tablespoons margarine, melted

Preheat oven to 500°. In a shallow pan, combine sour cream, lemon juice, and chili powder. Dip fish into sour cream mixture and coat with chips. Place fish in a greased 13 x 9 inch baking dish. Pour margarine over fish. Bake at 500° for 10 to 15 minutes. Makes 2 servings.

BAKED SALMON LOAF

1 (14.75 ounce) can pink salmon

20 saltine crackers, crushed

2 eggs, beaten

2½ *tablespoons grated Parmesan cheese*

2 tablespoons lemon juice

Preheat oven to 350°. In a large bowl, combine all ingredients, mixing well. Shape into loaf. Using an 8 x 4 x 2 inch loaf pan, bake at 350° for 35 minutes. Makes 4 servings.

TO REMOVE THE FISHY TASTE, SOAK RAW FISH IN A QUART OF WATER AND TWO TABLESPOONS OF BAKING SODA FOR A HALF-HOUR. RINSE AND PAT DRY BEFORE COOKING.

IRRESISTIBLE SALMON LOAF

4 eggs

2 cups milk

1 (10¾ ounce) can cream of mushroom soup

1 (6 ounce) package Caesar style croutons

1 (14.75 ounce) can salmon

½ cup chopped green pepper

¼ cup diced onion

2 tablespoons grated Parmesan cheese

Preheat oven to 350°. Coat a 2 quart baking dish with non-stick cooking spray. In a medium bowl, beat eggs, milk, and soup. Add croutons, salmon, green pepper, and onion, mixing well. Pour mixture into prepared baking dish. Sprinkle with Parmesan cheese. Bake at 350° for 50 minutes. Makes 6 servings.

FRIED SALMON PATTIES

Super-Fast

1 (14.75 ounce) can pink salmon

20 saltine crackers, crushed

2 eggs, beaten

1 tablespoon lemon juice

⅓ cup vegetable oil

In a large bowl, combine salmon, cracker crumbs, eggs, and lemon juice. Shape into patties. Heat oil in a large skillet, fry salmon patties until golden brown. Makes 4 to 6 servings.

COCONUT SHRIMP

1 cup flour

1 cup beer

1 pound medium shrimp

1 (14 ounce) package shredded coconut

1½ cups vegetable oil

In a medium bowl, combine flour and beer, mixing until batter is smooth. Dip shrimp into batter, then into shredded coconut. In a deep frying pan, heat oil to 375°. Fry shrimp in 2 or 3 batches without crowding. Cook until golden brown. Drain on paper towel. Makes 6 to 8 servings.

• •

DEEP FRIED OYSTERS

1 egg, slightly beaten

2 tablespoons water

½ cup cracker crumbs

½ teaspoon salt

½ teaspoon pepper

1 pint oysters, drained

Vegetable oil

In a small bowl, combine egg and water. Set aside. In a shallow pan, combine crumbs, salt, and pepper. Dip oysters in egg mixture, then in crumbs. Fry in deep oil until golden brown. Makes 4 servings.

SMOTHERED PHEASANT

⅓ cup vegetable oil

2 tablespoons margarine

6 pheasant halves

Salt and pepper to taste

1 (10¾ ounce) can cream of mushroom soup

1 (10¾ ounce) can cream of celery soup

1½ cups milk

Preheat oven to 350°. In a large skillet, heat oil and margarine. Brown pheasant. Place in a 2 quart baking dish, meat
side down. Salt and pepper to taste. In a medium bowl,
combine mushroom soup, celery soup, and milk. Pour over
pheasant. Cover and bake at 350° for 1 hour. Reduce heat to
300° and bake an additional 30 minutes. Makes 6 servings.

TENDER BAKED QUAIL

½ cup margarine

2 tablespoons vegetable oil

1 cup flour

Salt and pepper to taste

2 quail

2 cups light cream

Heat margarine and oil in a large skillet. In a small bowl,
combine flour, salt, and pepper. Dredge quail in flour mixture. Brown quail in oil. Remove from skillet and drain excess oil. Loosen crumbs in skillet and add cream, stirring
constantly. Return quail to skillet. Cover and simmer on
low heat. Add more cream as needed. Cook until tender.
Makes 2 servings.

GRILLED VENISON BURGERS

2 pounds ground venison

2 tablespoons horseradish

¼ cup ketchup

2 tablespoons Worcestershire sauce

Salt and pepper to taste

In a large bowl, combine all ingredients and form into patties. Grill to desired doneness. Makes 8 servings.

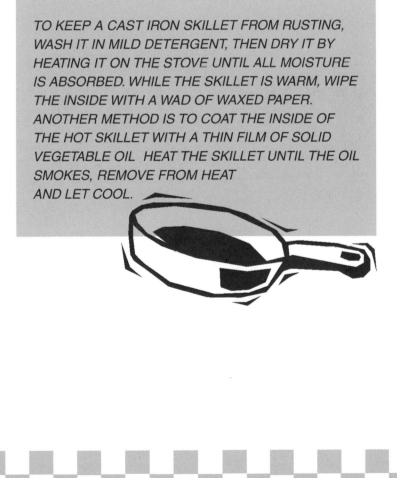

TO KEEP A CAST IRON SKILLET FROM RUSTING, WASH IT IN MILD DETERGENT, THEN DRY IT BY HEATING IT ON THE STOVE UNTIL ALL MOISTURE IS ABSORBED. WHILE THE SKILLET IS WARM, WIPE THE INSIDE WITH A WAD OF WAXED PAPER. ANOTHER METHOD IS TO COAT THE INSIDE OF THE HOT SKILLET WITH A THIN FILM OF SOLID VEGETABLE OIL HEAT THE SKILLET UNTIL THE OIL SMOKES, REMOVE FROM HEAT AND LET COOL.

STEAK AND PORK MARINADE

2 cloves garlic, minced

½ cup vegetable oil

3 tablespoons soy sauce

2 tablespoons ketchup

1 tablespoon vinegar

½ teaspoon fresh pepper

In a small bowl, combine all ingredients, mixing well. Pour over your favorite meat. Cover and refrigerate for 8 hours for best flavor. Makes 1 cup.

COOK OUT STEAK SAUCE

Super-Fast

1 (12 ounce) bottle chili sauce

1 (14 ounce) bottle ketchup

1 (11 ounce) bottle A-1® Sauce

1 (10 ounce) bottle Worcestershire sauce

1 (16 ounce) bottle chutney

Tabasco® to taste

Using a blender, combine all ingredients until smooth. This sauce is delicious!

FAVORITE HORSERADISH MEAT SAUCE

1 cup whipping cream

3 tablespoons horseradish

⅛ teaspoon salt

⅛ teaspoon pepper

1 tablespoon sugar

Beat whipping cream until stiff. Fold in horseradish, salt, pepper, and sugar. Serve over your favorite meats.

• •

EASY BARBECUE SAUCE

1 (14 ounce) bottle hot style ketchup

3 tablespoons vinegar

2 teaspoons celery seed

1 clove garlic, halved

In a small bowl, combine ketchup, vinegar, celery seed, and garlic. Cover and refrigerate for several hours. Discard garlic. Baste meat during last 10 minutes of grilling. Makes 1½ cups.

• •

PINEAPPLE ORANGE BASTING SAUCE

Super-Fast

½ (6 ounce can) frozen pineapple

¼ cup orange marmalade

2 tablespoons steak sauce

In a small saucepan, combine pineapple juice, marmalade, and steak sauce. Cook and stir over medium heat until mixture is hot. Use sauce to baste poultry or pork during the last 10 to15 minutes of grilling. Makes ⅔ cup.

113

PAPRIKA SWISS STEAK

Vegetable cooking spray

1 pound sirloin steak, cut ¾ inch thick

¼ teaspoon salt

1 (14½ ounce) can stewed tomatoes, undrained

1 tablespoon paprika

2 tablespoons ketchup

¼ teaspoon caraway seeds

Coat a medium skillet with non-stick vegetable cooking spray. Cook beef over medium heat until brown. Add salt, tomatoes, paprika, ketchup, and caraway seeds. Mix well. Reduce heat. Cover and simmer for 20 minutes. Makes 4 servings.

Per Serving: Calories-190, Protein-23 gm, Fat-5 gm, Carbohydrates-14 gm, Cholesterol-65 mg, Sodium-530 mg.

CAST IRON SKILLET STEAK

Super-Fast

Vegetable cooking spray

1 pound flank steak, well trimmed

½ teaspoon salt

¾ teaspoon crushed rosemary

¼ teaspoon ground black pepper

Spray a 10 inch cast iron skillet with cooking spray. Heat skillet until hot. Meanwhile, rub steak with salt, rosemary, and pepper. Add steak to hot skillet, reduce heat to medium. Cook until desired doneness. Thinly slice before serving. Makes 4 servings.

Per Serving: Calories-200, Protein-28 gm, Fat-9 gm, Carbohydrates-1 gram, Cholesterol-47 mg, Sodium-330 mg.

BIT OF A KICK PORK CHOPS

4 pork loin chops, ½ inch thick

3 tablespoons reduced sodium soy sauce

3 tablespoons ketchup

2 teaspoons honey

Preheat oven to 350°. Place pork chops in an 8 x 8 x 2 inch baking dish. In a small bowl, mix soy sauce, ketchup, and honey. Pour over pork. Cover and bake at 350° for 45 minutes. Uncover and bake 6 additional minutes. Makes 4 servings.

Per Serving: Calories-190, Protein-22 gm, Fat-8 gm, Carbohydrates-19 gm, Cholesterol-65 mg, Sodium-145 mg.

• •

GRILLED HONEY PORK CHOPS

¼ cup honey

2 tablespoons Dijon mustard

1 tablespoon orange juice

1 teaspoon cider vinegar

½ teaspoon Worcestershire sauce

4 boneless butterfly pork loin chops, cut 1 inch thick

In a small bowl, combine honey, mustard, orange juice, vinegar, and Worcestershire sauce. Brush mixture over pork chops and grill 14 to 16 minutes, brushing occasionally with mixture. Makes 4 servings.

Per Serving: Calories-235, Protein-22 gm, Fat-8 gm, Carbohydrates-19 gm, Cholesterol-65 mg, Sodium-145 mg.

BACKYARD GRILLED PORK TENDERLOIN

¼ cup fresh lemon juice

2 tablespoons chopped fresh oregano

2 tablespoons fresh parsley

2 (¾ pound each) pork tenderloins

1 tablespoon olive oil

½ teaspoon salt

¼ teaspoon pepper

In a plastic bag, combine lemon juice, oregano, parsley, tenderloins, and olive oil. Seal and turn to coat. Marinate 30 minutes. Remove tenderloin. Salt and pepper meat. Place tenderloins on grill over medium heat and cook to desired doneness. Thinly slice before serving. Makes 6 servings.

Per Serving: Calories-225, Protein-27 gm, Fat-12 gm, Carbohydrates-1 gram, Cholesterol-71 mg, Sodium-245 mg.

SKILLET COOKED CHICKEN BREAST

4 skinless, boneless chicken
    breast halves

¼ cup chicken broth

1 tablespoon lemon juice

¼ teaspoon salt

In a 10 inch nonstick skillet, combine all ingredients. Heat to boiling. Reduce heat, cover and simmer 10 to 15 minutes or until chicken is done. Makes 4 servings.

Per Serving: Calories-140, Protein-25 gm, Fat-4 gm, Carbohydrates-1 gm, Cholesterol-70 mg, Sodium-210 mg.

CRISPY BAKED CHICKEN

Vegetable cooking spray

1 egg white

½ cup crushed reduced-fat wheat thin crackers

½ cup grated Parmesan cheese

2 boneless, skinless chicken breasts

Preheat oven to 350°. Spray a cookie sheet with vegetable cooking spray. Set aside. In a shallow bowl, beat egg white. Set aside. Using a shallow pan or plate, combine crackers and cheese. Dip chicken in egg white, then roll in cracker mixture. Place chicken on prepared cookie sheet. Bake at 350° for 35 to 40 minutes. Makes 2 servings.

Per Serving: Calories-329, Protein-35 gm, Fat-11 gm, Carbohydrates-20 gm, Cholesterol-75 mg, Sodium-570 mg.

SAUCY SWEET AND SOUR CHICKEN

Vegetable cooking spray

1 pound cooked chicken, cut into 1 inch pieces

4 cups assorted vegetables

1 (8 ounce) can pineapple chunks, drained

½ cup sweet and sour sauce

Coat a 12 inch skillet with vegetable cooking spray. Heat skillet and add vegetables, stirring for 2 minutes. Add chicken and sweet and sour sauce. Cook and stir until mixture is hot. Serve over noodles or rice. Makes 4 servings.

Per Serving: Calories-230, Protein-26 gm, Fat-5 gm, Carbohydrates-23 gm, Cholesterol-70 mg, Sodium-190 mg.

CHICKEN BARBECUED TWIST

4 skinless, boneless chicken breast halves

½ cup Hoisin sauce

1 tablespoon sesame oil

1 tablespoon tomato paste

½ teaspoon ground ginger

2 cloves garlic, crushed

Place chicken breasts on rack in broiler pan. In a small bowl, mix remaining ingredients, brush over chicken. Broil 4 inches from heat for 7 to 8 minutes. Brush with sauce. Turn and broil 5 additional minutes or until chicken is done. Heat remaining sauce to boiling. Serve with chicken. Makes 4 servings.

Per Serving: Calories-175, Protein-27 gm, Fat-5 gm, Carbohydrates-2 gm, Cholesterol-7 mg, Sodium-150 mg.

● ●

BAKED CHICKEN AND PEPPERS

2 skinless, boneless chicken breasts, cut in half

2 green peppers, chopped

⅓ cup low-sodium soy sauce

Super-Fast

Preheat oven to 350°. Use an 11 x 7 x 2 inch baking pan and arrange chicken in bottom of pan. Top with green peppers. Pour soy sauce over chicken. Cover and bake at 350° for 35 minutes, or until chicken is cooked. Makes 4 servings.

Per Serving: Calories-144, Protein-27 gm, Fat-2 gm, Carbohydrates-4 gm, Cholesterol-65 mg, Sodium-873 mg.

TASTY ORANGE CHICKEN

Vegetable cooking spray

4 boneless and skinless chicken breasts

4 teaspoons Dijon mustard

½ onion, diced

1 cup orange juice

2 teaspoons butter

2 tablespoons brown sugar

Preheat oven to 350°. Coat an 11 x 7 x 2 inch baking pan with vegetable cooking spray. Place chicken in prepared pan. Coat chicken with mustard. Cover with onion. Pour orange juice over chicken. Place ½ teaspoon butter on each chicken breast. Bake at 350° for 25 minutes. Sprinkle brown sugar over chicken and bake an additional 15 minutes. Makes 4 servings.

Per Serving: Calories-136, Protein-26 gm, Fat-2 gm, Carbohydrates-5 gm, Cholesterol-65 mg, Sodium-74 mg.

IF YOU BURN YOUR TONGUE ON HOT FOOD, PLACE A LITTLE SUGAR ON YOUR TONGUE. AS THE SUGAR DISSOLVES, IT WILL TAKE AWAY THE BURN.

SLIM AND TRIM CHICKEN STIR FRY

1 pound boneless and skinless chicken breasts
Vegetable cooking spray
½ cup teriyaki baste and glaze sauce
3 tablespoons lemon juice
1 (16 ounce) package frozen mixed vegetables
Hot rice, if desired

Cut chicken into bite sized pieces. Coat a 12 inch skillet with vegetable cooking spray. Cook and stir chicken over medium heat. Add sauce, lemon juice, and frozen vegetables. Cover and simmer until vegetables are coated and crisp tender. Serve over rice, if desired. Makes 4 servings.

Per Serving: Calories-205, Protein-29 gm, Fat-4 gm, Carbohydrates-16 gm, Cholesterol-70 mg, Sodium-1470 mg.

WHEN PREPARING STUFFING FOR A TURKEY, ALLOW ONE CUP OF STUFFING FOR EACH POUND OF MEAT. A ONE POUND LOAF OF BREAD MAKES 8 CUPS OF BREAD CRUMBS.

SOUTHWESTERN CHICKEN

Super-Fast

Vegetable cooking spray

1 pound boneless and skinless chicken breast halves

1 (14½ ounce) can chunky style salsa

1 (15 ounce) can spicy chili beans

½ cup shredded reduced-fat Cheddar cheese

Coat a 12 inch non-stick skillet with vegetable cooking spray. Heat skillet over medium heat, before adding chicken. Cook chicken until light brown. Add salsa and beans. Reduce heat. Cook uncovered 15 minutes, stirring often. Sprinkle each serving with 2 tablespoons cheese. Makes 4 servings.

Per Serving: Calories-245, Protein-34 gm, Fat-5 gm, Carbohydrates-21 gm, Cholesterol-70 mg, Sodium-1070 mg.

TURKEY SMOTHERED IN SAUCE

Vegetable cooking spray

1 pound turkey breast

⅓ cup orange marmalade

½ teaspoon ground ginger

1 teaspoon Worcestershire sauce

Coat a medium skillet with vegetable cooking spray. Brown turkey breast. Add marmalade, ginger, and Worcestershire sauce. Cover and simmer for 15 minutes, stirring occasionally. Cut into thin slices. Spoon sauce over turkey before serving. Makes 4 servings.

Per Serving: Calories-175, Protein-27 gm, Fat-1 gm, Carbohydrates-16 gm, Cholesterol-75 mg, Sodium-65 mg.

FRIED HALIBUT FILLETS

¾ cup dried bread crumbs

2 tablespoons grated Parmesan cheese

2 tablespoons chopped fresh parsley

1 teaspoon paprika

4 (4 ounce) fresh halibut fillets

2 egg whites, slightly beaten

Vegetable cooking spray

In a shallow dish, combine bread crumbs with cheese, parsley, and paprika. Dip fillet into beaten egg whites, then in bread crumbs. Place in a single layer on waxed paper and place in freezer for 1 hour. Spray a large skillet with vegetable cooking spray. Add fillets. Cook over medium-high heat until brown on both sides. Makes 4 servings.

Per Serving: Calories-157, Protein-20 gm, Fat-2 gm, Carbohydrates-12 gm, Cholesterol-67 mg, Sodium-248 mg.

• •

CHINESE STYLE FLOUNDER

2 tablespoons soy sauce

2 tablespoons seasoned rice vinegar

4 (6 ounce) flounder fillets

2 teaspoons grated ginger

2 green onions, chopped

Preheat oven to 425°. In a small bowl, mix soy sauce and vinegar. Place each fillet on a 15 x 12 inch piece of aluminum foil. Spread fish with ginger. Spoon one tablespoon of soy sauce mixture on top. Sprinkle with green onions. Fold foil over fish and seal edges. Bake at 425° for 8 to 10 minutes. Makes 4 servings.

Per Serving: Calories-175, Protein-33 gm, Fat-2 gm, Carbohydrates-5 gm, Cholesterol-90 mg, Sodium-855 mg.

LOUISIANA OVEN-FRIED CATFISH

Butter-flavored cooking spray

¼ cup buttermilk or skim milk

1 egg white, slightly beaten

⅓ cup yellow cornmeal

⅓ cup bread crumbs

1 teaspoon Cajun Creole seasoning

1 pound catfish

Preheat oven to 500°. Spray a 13 x 9 inch cookie sheet with butter-flavored cooking spray. Set aside. In a small bowl, combine buttermilk and egg white. In a separate bowl, combine cornmeal, bread crumbs, and seasoning. Cut catfish into 2 x 1½ inch pieces. Dip fish in buttermilk mixture, then in cornmeal mixture. Place in prepared pan. Bake for 10 minutes or until fish is flaky. Makes 4 servings.

Per Serving: Calories-190, Protein-28 gm, Fat-2 gm, Carbohydrates-16 gm, Cholesterol-70 mg, Sodium-220 mg.

QUICK-FIX SALMON STEAKS

4 salmon steaks, 1 inch thick

1 teaspoon oil

⅛ teaspoon salt

⅛ teaspoon pepper

Preheat broiler. Brush oil on both sides of salmon steaks and sprinkle with salt and pepper. Place salmon on rack in broiling pan and broil 4 inches from heat until salmon is done, turn once. Makes 4 servings.

Per Serving: Calories-284, Protein-30 gm, Fat-17 gm, Carbohydrates-0 mg, Cholesterol-88 mg, Sodium-123 mg.

Heart of the Matter

(Vegetables, Pasta, Rice, and Casseroles)

SPECIAL GREEN BEAN CASSEROLE

1 (15 ounce) can green beans, drained

1 teaspoon soy sauce

1 (10¾ ounce) can cream of mushroom soup

1 (2.8 ounce) can French fried onions

1 tablespoon Cheez Whiz ®

Preheat oven to 350°. Combine green beans, soy sauce, soup, ½ can of onions, and Cheez Whiz®. Mix well. Pour into 1½ quart baking dish. Bake at 350° for 20 minutes. Remove from oven. Top with remaining onions. Bake for 10 minutes or until onions are golden brown. Makes 8 servings.

• •

GOOD OLD NAVY BEANS

2 pounds white navy beans

1 generous ham hock

1 whole onion, peeled

Salt and pepper to taste

¼ cup butter

Soak beans 8-10 hours in cold water. Drain. In a large saucepan, cover beans with fresh water and bring to a boil. Add ham hock, onion, salt, and pepper. Simmer over low heat for about 4 hours. Add more water when needed. Add butter after beans are cooked. Makes 6 servings.

STORE FRESH ASPARAGUS CUT SIDE DOWN IN A PITCHER CONTAINING AN INCH OF WATER. REFRIGERATE UNTIL READY TO USE. REPLACE WATER AS NEEDED FOR FRESHNESS.

AMERICAN BAKED BEANS

2 (8 ounce) cans pork and beans

½ cup packed brown sugar

½ cup chopped onion

1 teaspoon Worcestershire sauce

3 tablespoons maple syrup

2 tablespoons ketchup

3 bacon slices

Preheat oven to 350°. In a large bowl, combine beans, brown sugar, onions, Worcestershire sauce, syrup, ketchup, and bacon. Mix well. Pour into a baking dish. Bake at 350° for 35 minutes. Makes 4 to 6 servings.

GLAZED CARROT STRIPS

1½ pounds raw carrots

⅓ cup packed brown sugar

½ teaspoon grated orange peel

2½ tablespoons butter

In a medium saucepan, cook carrots in a small amount of water until just tender. Drain carrots and cut into strips. In same saucepan, mix brown sugar, orange peel, and butter. Add carrots. Cook over low heat, stirring occasionally, until carrots are glazed (about 5 minutes). Makes 4 to 6 servings.

PEEL AND SLICE ORANGE CARROTS

¼ cup butter

2 tablespoons maple syrup

1 tablespoon sugar

1 cup orange juice

1 pound carrots, peeled and sliced

Melt butter in a medium saucepan. Add syrup, sugar, orange juice, and carrots. Cover and simmer over low heat for 15 to 20 minutes or until carrots are tender. Uncover and cook until liquid is absorbed. Makes 4 servings.

• •

DROP BY THE SPOONFUL CORN

1 (15 ounce) can whole kernel corn, drained

1 egg, beaten

1 tablespoon flour

½ teaspoon salt

½ teaspoon sugar

¼ cup margarine

In a large bowl, combine corn, egg, flour, salt, and sugar. Set aside. In a medium skillet, heat margarine until hot. Drop mixture by teaspoonfuls into hot margarine. Brown carefully on both sides. Reduce heat and cook 6 minutes. Makes 4 to 6 servings.

SWEET CORN IN CREAM

12 ears of corn

¼ cup butter, melted

½ cup cream

Salt and pepper to taste

Remove kernels from corn. In a large saucepan, combine corn, butter, cream, salt, and pepper. Cook for 10 minutes until corn is tender. Makes 6 to 8 servings.

• •

FRIED CUCUMBERS

½ cup flour

½ cup finely crushed cracker crumbs

1 egg

½ cup milk

2 cucumbers, peeled and sliced

⅓ cup margarine

In a small bowl, combine flour with cracker crumbs. Pour onto a plate and set aside. In another bowl, beat egg and milk. Soak cucumbers in milk, a few at a time. Dredge cucumbers in cracker mix until coated on both sides. Melt margarine in skillet. Fry cucumbers in margarine until golden brown. Sprinkle with salt, if desired. Makes 2 servings.

QUICKLY REMOVE THE SILK FROM AN EAR OF CORN BY RUBBING WITH A DRY PIECE OF NYLON NET.

NOT JUST CABBAGE

1 small head red cabbage, thinly sliced

3 medium apples, peeled, cored, grated

¾ cup sugar

½ cup red wine vinegar

1 teaspoon cloves

In crock pot, combine all ingredients. Mix well. Cover. Cook on low 6 hours. Makes 4 to 6 servings.

• •

PEAS AU GRATIN

3 cups peas

1 (2.5 ounce) can water chestnuts, drained and sliced

Super-Fast

1 (10¾ ounce) can cream of mushroom soup

1½ cups grated Cheddar cheese

Preheat oven to 350°. In a large bowl, combine peas and water chestnuts. Add soup, mixing well. Add cheese, mixing well. Pour mixture into a lightly greased baking dish. Bake at 350° for 30 minutes. Makes 6 to 8 servings.

IF YOU ADD TOO MUCH VINEGAR TO A RECIPE, A PINCH OF BAKING SODA WILL COUNTERACT THE EXCESS ACIDITY.

FOR SPINACH LOVERS

*3 (10 ounce) packages frozen spinach, thawed
and drained*

2 cups cottage cheese

1 cup grated cheddar cheese

3 eggs

¼ cup flour

1 teaspoon salt

½ cup butter or margarine, melted

In large bowl, combine all ingredients. Mix well. Pour mixture into crock pot. Cover. Cook on high 1 hour. Reduce heat to low and cook 4 hours. Makes 6 to 8 servings.

• •

BAKED CREAM SPINACH

2 pounds fresh spinach

1 (8 ounce) package cream cheese, softened

1 stick butter, melted

¼ teaspoon nutmeg

Salt and pepper to taste

Preheat oven to 350°. Wash spinach and remove stems. Dry on paper towels. In a large bowl, combine cream cheese, butter, nutmeg, salt, and pepper. Fold in spinach. Pour into a 2 quart baking dish. Bake at 350° for 30 minutes. Makes 6 to 8 servings.

POTATOES WITH STYLE

1¼ cups milk

1 (8 ounce) package cream cheese

1 tablespoon chives

½ teaspoon instant minced onion

¼ teaspoon salt

3 cups cubed cooked potatoes

Paprika

Preheat oven to 350°. In a large saucepan, blend milk into cream cheese, cook and stir over low heat until blended. Add chives, onions and salt. Add cubed potatoes, stirring to coat. Pour mixture into a 2 quart baking dish. Sprinkle with paprika. Bake at 350° for 30 minutes. Makes 4 to 6 servings.

• •

QUICK AND TASTY POTATOES

Super-Fast

4 tablespoons margarine

1 small onion, sliced

1 (10¾ ounce) can broccoli cheese soup

¾ cup milk

4 medium potatoes, cooked and sliced

In a large saucepan, melt margarine. Add onion and cook until tender. Stir in soup and milk. Bring to a full boil. Reduce heat and add potatoes, stirring to coat, and simmer for 5 minutes until potatoes are heated. Makes 6 to 8 servings.

TWICE BAKED POTATOES

4 large baking potatoes
Solid shortening
Milk
Butter
Salt and pepper to taste
½ cup sour cream
1 cup shredded Cheddar cheese

Preheat oven to 350°. Rub potatoes with shortening for softer skins. Bake at 375° until potatoes are done. Remove from oven. Cut potatoes in half (lengthwise). Scoop out inside, leaving a thin shell. Mash potatoes with milk, butter, salt, and pepper, until fluffy. Add sour cream. Blend well. Fill shells with mashed potatoes, top with Cheddar cheese. Bake at 350° for 15 to 20 minutes. Makes 8 servings.

• •

MASHED TATER PATTIES

1 egg, beaten
3 cups mashed potatoes
¼ cup flour
¼ cup chopped onion
¼ cup margarine

In a large bowl, mix egg, potatoes, flour, and onion, shaping into patties. Dot patties with margarine. Place under broiler, turning when brown. Or, fry in margarine until brown. Makes 4 to 6 servings.

SPECTACULAR SPUDS

4 servings instant mashed potatoes

½ cup whipping cream

1 teaspoon sugar

½ teaspoon onion powder

⅓ cup grated Parmesan cheese

Place mixing bowl for whipping cream into refrigerator to chill. Preheat oven to 350°. Prepare potatoes according to package directions. Spoon potatoes into ungreased 1½ quart baking dish. Using chilled mixing bowl, beat whipping cream, sugar, and onion powder until soft peaks form. Spread over potatoes. Sprinkle with cheese. Bake at 350° for 30 minutes or until golden brown. Makes 4 servings.

• •

OLD TIMER'S SCALLOPED POTATOES

6 medium potatoes, peeled and sliced

1½ cups cubed ham

4 tablespoons butter

4 tablespoons flour

Salt and pepper to taste

2 cups milk

Preheat oven to 350°. In a large mixing bowl, combine potato slices and ham cubes. Place in a 2 quart baking dish. In a small saucepan, mix butter, flour, salt, and pepper. Cook on low for 2 minutes. Add milk. Continue to cook and stir until mixture thickens. Pour milk mixture over potatoes. Bake at 350° for 1 hour. Makes 6 servings.

MICROWAVE AU GRATIN POTATOES

4 medium potatoes

2 tablespoons water

½ cup chopped onion

1 celery stalk, chopped

Salt

⅓ pound Velveeta® cheese, sliced

2 tablespoons milk

Peel and slice potatoes. In a microwave-safe bowl, layer half the potatoes, add water. Layer onion and celery and sprinkle with salt. Top with remaining potatoes. Cover with plastic wrap. Microwave 15 minutes or until potatoes are tender. Top potatoes with sliced cheese and milk. Microwave until cheese melts. Makes 4 servings.

Super-Fast

MAKE A HIT HASH BROWNS

1 (2 pound) package frozen hash browns

1 cup sour cream

½ cup chopped onions

1 teaspoon salt

1 (10¾ ounce) can cream of celery soup

2 cups grated Cheddar cheese

¼ cup butter, melted

2 cups crushed corn flakes

Preheat oven to 350°. Combine hash browns, sour cream, onion, salt, soup, and cheese. Pour mixture into a 13 x 9 inch baking dish. Top with melted butter, then corn flakes. Bake at 350° for 1 hour. Makes 6 to 8 servings.

CHEESY HASH BROWN POTATOES

½ cup butter, melted

1 (2 pound) package frozen hash browns

2 cups grated cheese

2 cups cream of chicken soup

1 pint sour cream

½ cup chopped onion

Salt and pepper to taste

Preheat oven to 350°. Pour melted butter into a 13 x 9 inch baking dish. In a large mixing bowl, combine potatoes, cheese, soup, sour cream, onion, salt, and pepper. Pour mixture into 13 x 9 inch baking dish. Bake at 350° for 45 minutes. Makes 6 servings.

• •

GLAZED SWEET POTATOES

4 or 5 sweet potatoes or yams, cooked, reserve one
    cup of cooking water

½ cup maple syrup

2 tablespoons brown sugar

1 teaspoon sugar

3 tablespoons butter

Preheat oven to 350°. Place cooked sweet potatoes in a 2 quart baking dish. In a small saucepan, combine cooking water from potatoes, syrup, brown sugar, sugar, and butter. Bring to a boil, lower heat and simmer for 2 minutes. Pour over potatoes. Bake at 350° for 25 minutes. Makes 6 to 8 servings.

SKILLET CARAMEL SWEET POTATOES

1 cup packed brown sugar

¼ cup butter

¼ cup water

½ teaspoon salt

4 cooked sweet potatoes

Super-Fast

In a large skillet, mix brown sugar, butter, water, and salt. Bring to a boil. Add sweet potatoes and simmer over low heat for 15 minutes or until potatoes have a caramel-like glaze. Makes 6 servings.

• •

ZUCCHINI IN A SKILLET

½ cup chopped onion

1 tablespoon margarine

2 medium zucchini, sliced

2 tomatoes, chopped

¼ teaspoon oregano

Salt and pepper to taste

In a large skillet, brown onion in margarine. Add zucchini, tomatoes, oregano, salt, and pepper. Cover and simmer on low heat until zucchini is tender. Makes 4 to 6 servings.

REMOVE COOKED SQUASH FROM THE SHELL BY USING AN ICE CREAM SCOOP.

ITALIAN STYLE ZUCCHINI

4 cups sliced zucchini

4 cups canned tomatoes

1 onion, sliced

½ teaspoon Italian seasoning

Salt and pepper to taste

¼ cup Parmesan cheese

Preheat oven to 350°. Spray a 2 quart baking dish with non-stick cooking spray. Alternately layer zucchini, tomatoes, and onions until all ingredients are used. Sprinkle with Italian seasoning, salt, and pepper. Top with Parmesan cheese. Bake at 350° for 1 hour. Makes 6 servings.

CHICKEN VEGETABLE LINGUINI

1 (8 ounce) package linguini, cooked and
drained

2 cups cooked mixed vegetables

2 cups cooked chicken, cubed

1 cup Ranch style dressing

1 tablespoon grated Parmesan cheese

In a large saucepan, combine linguini, vegetables, chicken, and Ranch dressing. Heat thoroughly. Sprinkle with Parmesan cheese before serving. Makes 6 to 8 servings.

TO RIPEN TOMATOES IN A HURRY, PLACE THEM IN A CONTAINER WITH OTHER FRUIT, ESPECIALLY PEARS.

FETTUCINE ALFREDO

1 (8 ounce) package fettucine

1 cup heavy cream

2 cloves garlic, crushed

8 slices of bacon, cooked and crumbled

¼ cup parsley, chopped

¼ cup grated Parmesan cheese

Prepare fettuccine according to package directions. Drain. In a large saucepan, heat cream and garlic, but do not boil. Add pasta, bacon, and parsley. Mix well. Sprinkle with Parmesan cheese before serving. Makes 4 servings.

BROILED CHEESE RAVIOLI

1 (30 ounce) package ravioli

1 (10¾ ounce) can Cheddar cheese soup

1¼ cups milk

1 cup shredded mozzarella cheese

1 teaspoon Italian seasoning

Parmesan cheese

Prepare ravioli according to package directions. Place ravioli in ungreased baking dish. In a small saucepan, heat soup and milk until hot. Add mozzarella cheese and Italian seasoning. Cook and stir over low heat, until cheese melts. Pour mixture over ravioli. Sprinkle with Parmesan cheese. Broil 3 to 4 inches from heat until cheese is light brown. Makes 6 servings.

HOMEMADE MACARONI AND CHEESE

1 (16 ounce) package macaroni

2 tablespoons butter

½ tablespoon salt

1 (8 ounce) box Velveeta® cheese

2½ cups milk

Preheat oven to 350°. Prepare macaroni according to package directions, drain. In same saucepan, combine butter, salt, cheese, and milk. Heat until cheese melts. Stir often to keep sauce from scorching. Add macaroni and stir until coated with cheese. Bake at 350° for 40 minutes. Makes 8 servings.

• •

HOT VEGGIE CASSEROLE

1 (16 ounce) package frozen mixed broccoli and
    cauliflower

1 cup frozen green beans

1 cup chopped onion

Salt and pepper

8 ounces Velveeta® cheese, cut into cubes

1 (10¾ ounce) can cream of celery soup

1 (2.8 ounce) can French fried onions

Preheat oven to 350°. Lightly butter a 13 x 9 inch baking dish. Layer broccoli/cauliflower mix on bottom of dish. Add layer of green beans, then onion. Salt and pepper to taste. In a medium saucepan, melt cheese in soup, stirring to keep mixture from burning. Pour cheese mixture over vegetables. Bake at 350° for 45 minutes. Remove from oven. Top with French fried onions. Bake for 5 minutes, or until onions are golden brown. Makes 8 servings.

LIGHT AND CHEESY CABBAGE CASSEROLE

2 cups crushed corn flakes

½ cup butter, melted

4 cups cooked cabbage, shredded

1 cup milk

1 cup grated Cheddar cheese

½ cup mayonnaise

1 (10¾ ounce) can cream of celery soup

Preheat oven to 350°. In a large bowl, mix corn flakes and butter. Spread half the mixture in a lightly buttered baking dish. Add cabbage. In a medium bowl, combine milk, cheese, mayonnaise, and soup. Pour over cabbage. Top with remaining corn flakes. Bake at 350° for 30 minutes. Makes 6 servings.

BAKED CHICKEN NOODLE CASSEROLE

1 (8 ounce) package noodles, cooked

4 cups cooked chicken, diced

1 (10¾ ounce) can cream of mushroom soup

½ cup milk

1 cup grated cheese

1 cup buttered bread crumbs

Preheat oven to 350°. In a large bowl, combine noodles, chicken, soup, milk, and cheese. Mix well. Pour into 13 x 9 inch baking dish. Top with crumbs. Bake at 350° for 20 minutes. Makes 6 servings.

STORE CRUSHED POTATO CHIPS IN A PLASTIC BAG IN THE FREEZER FOR USE AS CASSEROLE TOPPINGS.

A WILD RICE AND CHICKEN CASSEROLE

2 cups cooked chicken, cubed

2 cups cooked wild rice

¼ cup chopped green pepper

1 (10¾ ounce) can cream of mushroom soup

½ cup milk

Salt and pepper to taste

Preheat oven to 350°. In a large bowl, combine all ingredients, mixing well. Pour into a 2 quart baking dish. Bake at 350° for 30 minutes. Makes 6 servings.

• •

PENNY SAVER BEEF CASSEROLE

1½ pounds ground beef

1 cup chopped onion

1 (8 ounce) package cream cheese

1 (10¾ ounce) can cream of mushroom soup

¼ cup milk

1 teaspoon salt

¼ cup ketchup

1 (10 count) can refrigerated biscuits

Preheat oven to 350°. In a large skillet, brown ground beef and onions. Drain on paper towels to remove fat. Return to skillet. Add cream cheese, soup, milk, salt, and ketchup, mixing well. Pour into a 2 quart baking dish. Bake at 350° for 10 minutes. Remove from heat. Place biscuits around outer edge of baking dish. Return to oven for 15 to 20 minutes or until biscuits are brown. Makes 6 to 8 servings

COMPANY PORK CHOP CASSEROLE

6 pork chops

4 potatoes, cooked, cubed

2 (15 ounce) cans green beans, drained

1½ cups milk

4 tablespoons flour

Butter

Preheat oven to 350°. Lightly brown pork chops in non-stick cooking spray. Place 3 chops in a 2 quart baking dish, layer half the potatoes and half the green beans. Repeat. In a small bowl, combine milk and flour, mixing well. Pour milk mixture over pork chops, dotting with butter. Bake at 350° for 45 minutes or until chops are tender. Makes 6 servings.

• •

EASY TUNA CASSEROLE

Super-Fast

1 (7.25 ounce) box macaroni and cheese mix

1 (15 ounce) can peas

2 (6 ounce) cans tuna fish, drained

1 cup grated American cheese

Preheat oven to 375°. Prepare macaroni and cheese according to package directions. In same saucepan, combine macaroni and cheese, peas, tuna fish, and ½ cup cheese. Mix well. Place mixture in baking dish and top with remaining cheese. Bake at 375° for 35 minutes. .

TO KEEP CHEESE FROM STICKING, SPRAY GRATER WITH NON-STICK VEGETABLE SPRAY BEFORE USING.

TAMALE CASSEROLE

1 (15 ounce) can chili

7 tamales (fresh or canned),
   with husks removed

½ cup chopped onions

2 cups broken corn chips

1 cup grated Cheddar cheese

Preheat oven to 350°. Spread chili in a 2 quart baking dish.
Cut tamales into 1 inch pieces. Place tamale pieces on top
of chili. Layer onions, chips, and cheese. Bake at 350° for 30
minutes. Makes 6 servings

• •

ONE DISH POTATO DINNER

1½ cups ham, cubed

1 (10¾ ounce) can Cheddar cheese soup

½ cup sour cream

½ cup milk

1 cup frozen, mixed vegetables, thawed

4 potatoes, halved

Preheat oven to 350°. Spray a 2 quart baking dish with non-
stick cooking spray. Set aside. In a large saucepan, combine
ham, soup, sour cream, milk, and vegetables. Cook and stir
over medium heat until mixture is hot. Add potatoes and
stir to coat. Pour into baking dish. Bake at 350° for 2 hours.
Stir once during baking. Makes 4 servings.

*ABSORB ODORS WHILE COOKING CABBAGE BY
PLACING HALF A CUP OF VINEGAR ON THE STOVE
DURING COOKING.*

ONE POT CHICKEN AND NOODLES

2 cups cooked chicken, diced

3 cups cooked noodles

1 (10¾ ounce) can cream of chicken soup

½ cup milk

¾ cup grated Parmesan cheese

½ teaspoon pepper

In a large stew pot, combine all ingredients. Cook over medium heat, stirring occasionally. Makes 4 servings.

• •

NO MESS RICE CHICKEN DISH

1 (14½ ounce) can mixed vegetables

1 (10¾ ounce) can Cream of Mushroom soup

¾ cup uncooked white rice

1 cup water

4 skinless, boneless, chicken breast halves

Preheat oven to 400 degrees. In a 2 quart shallow baking dish, combine vegetables, soup, rice, and water. Place chicken on top of mixture. Cover and bake 45 to 50 minutes. Makes 4 servings.

10 MINUTE CHICKEN STEW

2 (12 ounce) jars chicken gravy

½ teaspoon poultry seasoning

3 cups cooked chicken strips

1 (14½ ounce) cans green beans, drained

1 (14½ ounce) can sliced carrots, drained

In a large skillet, combine gravy and poultry seasoning. Bring to a boil. Add chicken, green beans and carrots. Heat thoroughly. Makes 4 to 6 servings. This is great served over corn bread!

● ●

QUICK AND EASY CHICKEN POT PIE

1 (10¾ ounce) can cream of chicken soup

1 cup cooked chicken, chopped

1 (16 ounce) bag frozen vegetables

1¼ cups biscuit mix

½ cup milk

1 egg

Super-Fast

Preheat oven to 400°. Combine soup, chicken and vegetables. Pour into a 9-inch pie plate. Combine biscuit mix, milk, and egg. Pour over chicken mixture. Bake at 400° for 30 minutes. Makes 4 servings.

SOFT CHICKEN TACOS

*1 pound chicken breasts,
    boneless and skinless*

2 tablespoons cooking oil

2 cups water

1 cup mild salsa, chunky style

1 (1¼ ounce) package taco seasoning mix

2 cups instant rice, uncooked

8 to 12 flour tortillas

Grated Cheddar cheese for topping

Super-Fast

Cut chicken into strips. In a large skillet, brown chicken in oil. Drain on paper towels. Return to skillet. Add water, salsa, and seasoning mix. Stir and bring to a boil. Reduce heat to low. Add rice, cover. Cook for 5 minutes. Spoon mixture onto tortillas. Top with grated cheese. Fold in half. Makes 6 to 8 servings.

LIGHTER MASHED POTATOES COME FROM USING HOT MILK INSTEAD OF COLD MILK.

STUFFED GREEN PEPPERS

2 tablespoons olive oil

½ cup water

4 green peppers

1 pound ground beef

1 onion, chopped

1 tablespoon crushed garlic

¼ cup uncooked rice

2 tablespoons tomato paste

Preheat oven to 350°. Mix oil and water and pour into baking dish. Set aside. Remove tops from green peppers and scoop out seeds. Set Aside. Combine ground beef, onion, garlic, rice, and tomato paste. Stuff peppers with beef mixture and place in baking dish. Bake at 350° for 1 hour. Add more water if needed. Makes 4 servings.

ADD SEVERAL DROPS OF OIL TO YOUR SKILLET WHEN FRYING WITH BUTTER TO KEEP THE BUTTER FROM BURNING.

NOW THIS IS PIZZA BREAD

1 pound ground beef

1 pound Italian sausage

1 green pepper, chopped

1 (12 ounce) jar pizza sauce

1 loaf French bread

3 tablespoons grated Parmesan cheese

Mozzarella cheese, grated

Preheat oven to 350°. In a large skillet, fry meats and drain on paper towels. Return to skillet. Add green pepper and pizza sauce, mixing well. Slice bread in half, then split lengthwise. Spread meat mixture on bread. Top with cheese. Bake at 350° until cheese melts and bread is golden brown (about 15 minutes). Makes 4 servings.

• •

READY AND WAITING BEEF ON RICE

2 pounds beef, cubed

1 (10½ ounce) can beef broth

1 small onion, chopped

1 (10¾ ounce) can mushroom soup

3 tablespoons dry onion soup mix

In crock pot, combine all ingredients. Mix well. Cover. Cook on low 7 to 8 hours. Serve over rice. Makes 6 to 8 servings

GROUND BEEF AND CABBAGE SUPPER

1 pound ground beef

1 small onion, chopped

2 cups sliced potatoes

2 cups shredded cabbage

2 cups chopped celery

½ cup water

Salt

In a large skillet, fry ground beef and onion until meat is brown. Drain and return to skillet. Add potatoes, cabbage, celery, and water. Sprinkle with salt. Cover and simmer 20 minutes, or until vegetables are tender. Makes 6 to 8 servings.

ONE DISH HAMBURGER MEAL

1 pound ground beef

1 onion, chopped

2 tablespoons vegetable oil

1 (10¾ ounce) can cream of mushroom soup

1 cup grated Cheddar cheese

2 (15¼ ounce) cans green beans, drained

Preheat oven to 250°. In a large skillet, brown ground beef and onion in vegetable oil. Drain. In a large bowl, combine ground beef, soup, cheese, and green beans. Mix well and pour into a 13 x 9 inch baking dish. Cover and bake at 250° for 2 hours. Makes 4 to 6 servings. Makes 4 servings.

LAST MINUTE CHILI

1 (15 ounce) can chili with beans

1 small tomato, chopped

½ cup chopped onion

Corn chips

Super-Fast

In a small saucepan, combine all ingredients. Simmer over low heat for 15 minutes. Serve over corn chips. May also top with shredded cheese and additional chopped onion. Makes 2 servings.

• •

BEEF CHILI WITH A KICK

2 cups stew meat, cooked

1 (8 ounce) jar salsa

¼ cup chopped green onions

1 tablespoon chili powder

1 (15 ounce) can kidney beans, drained

Grated Cheddar cheese

In a medium saucepan, combine stew meat, salsa, onions, and chili powder. Cover and simmer for 10 minutes. Add kidney beans and heat thoroughly. Serve topped with grated Cheddar cheese. Makes 4 servings.

ELIMINATE COOKING ODORS FROM BROCCOLI, CAULIFLOWER, OR CABBAGE BY ADDING ONE OR TWO RIBS OF CELERY TO THE COOKING WATER.

OH WOW CHILI SKILLET BAKE

2 (15 ounce) cans chili with beans

½ cup Bisquick® mix

¼ cup milk

1 egg, beaten

1 cup shredded cheddar cheese

Preheat oven to 400 degrees. In medium saucepan, add chili; heat until hot, set aside. In medium bowl, combine Bisquik, milk, egg, and cheese. Mix well. In 2-quart casserole, pour in chili beans. Spoon Bisquick mixture in ring around outer edge of chili. Bake 20 minutes or until crust is golden brown. Makes 6 servings.

• •

JUST BEFORE PAYDAY CHILI

Super-Fast

½ pound ground beef

¼ cup chopped onion

1 (15 ounce) can chili with beans

1 (14½ ounce) can diced tomatoes, undrained

In a medium saucepan, brown ground beef and onion. Drain on paper towel and return to pan. Add chili and tomatoes. Simmer for 15 minutes. Makes 4 servings.

HOT'N HEARTY BEEF STEW

5 cups fresh vegetables (potatoes, carrots, onion, celery)

3 cups water

1 (1.5 ounce) package stew seasoning

2 pounds stew meat, cut into 1-inch cubes

¼ cup flour

In crock pot, combine vegetables, water, and seasoning. Mix well. Coat beef with flour and stir into mixture. Cover. Cook on low 7 to 8 hours or high 5 hours. Makes 6 servings.

• •

RED BEANS AND RICE

1 pound Polish sausage

2 (15-ounce) cans kidney beans

1 tablespoon Cajun seasoning

2 cups instant rice

Super-Fast

Cut sausage into 2 inch pieces. In a large saucepan, combine sausage, beans, and seasoning. Bring to a boil. Reduce heat and simmer for 20 minutes. Prepare rice according to package directions. Serve beans over rice. Makes 4 servings.

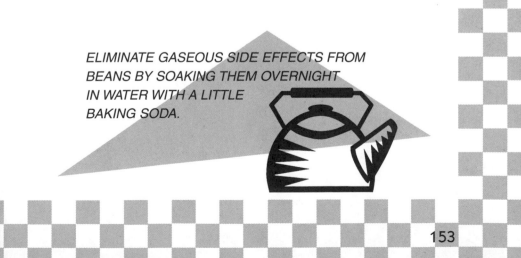

ELIMINATE GASEOUS SIDE EFFECTS FROM BEANS BY SOAKING THEM OVERNIGHT IN WATER WITH A LITTLE BAKING SODA.

MADE IN MINUTES EGGS BENEDICT

1 (.9 ounce) packet Hollandaise sauce

3 English muffins

1 pound ham, sliced into 6 pieces

6 eggs, poached

Super-Fast

Prepare Hollandaise sauce according to package directions. Keep warm. Toast English muffin halves. Heat ham slices in the microwave until hot (about 1 minute). Top each muffin half with a piece of ham and a poached egg. Pour warm Hollandaise sauce over poached egg. Makes 6 servings.

• •

ANYTIME SWISS CHEESE PIE

1⅔ cup milk

4 eggs

½ teaspoon salt

4 ounces smoked beef, sliced

1 cup shredded Swiss cheese

1 9-inch pie shell, unbaked

Preheat oven to 350°. In a large bowl, beat milk, eggs, and salt. Stir in beef and cheese. Pour into unbaked pie shell. Bake at 350° for 35 minutes. Allow pie to cool 5 minutes before serving. Makes 4 to 6 servings.

USE A VEGETABLE PEELER TO REMOVE TOUGH SCALES FROM THE LOWER PORTION OF ASPARAGUS STALKS.

BASIC SUNDAY MORNING OMELET

Super-Fast

4 eggs

2 tablespoons butter

½ cup grated cheese

½ cup diced ham

Beat eggs. Pour into heated skillet with butter. With a spatula, scrape the sides of the pan to keep eggs from sticking. When eggs are set, sprinkle cheese and ham over eggs. Carefully fold eggs in half. Slide omelet onto plate. Cut in half. Makes 2 servings.

• •

QUICHE FOR LUNCH

6 strips bacon, cooked and crumbled

1 9-inch pie crust, unbaked

1 cup grated Swiss cheese

3 eggs

2½ cups half and half

¼ teaspoon nutmeg

Salt and pepper to taste

Preheat oven to 350°. Place crumbled bacon in bottom of pie shell. Sprinkle with cheese. In a medium mixing bowl, beat eggs, half and half, nutmeg, salt, and pepper. Pour egg mixture into pie shell. Bake at 350° for 45 minutes, or until quiche is set. Makes 4 to 6 servings.

OVEN-COOKED RICE

1½ cups boiling water

1 tablespoon margarine

¾ cup long grain rice

½ teaspoon salt

Preheat oven to 350°. In a 1 quart baking dish, combine boiling water and margarine, mixing well. Stir in rice and salt. Cover. Bake at 350° for 35 minutes. Fluff with fork. Makes 4 servings

● ●

RICE AND RED BEANS SKILLET

1 tablespoon butter

½ cup sliced green onions

½ teaspoon minced garlic

2 cups cooked rice

1 cup fresh spinach leaves, torn into large pieces

1 can red beans, rinsed and drained

Melt butter in large skillet, add green onions and garlic. Cook over medium heat. Stir often, until onions are softened. Add rice, spinach and beans and cook until heated through. Season with salt and pepper. Makes 4 servings.

RICE WITH PECANS AND RAISINS

2 cups instant rice

2 cups chicken stock

1 cup raisins

1 cup pecans

In a large saucepan, cook rice in chicken stock. When rice is tender, stir in raisins and pecans. Makes 6 to 8 servings. A good side dish for turkey or chicken.

• •

FESTIVE CRANBERRY STUFFING

1¾ cups chicken broth

½ teaspoon pepper

1 stalk celery, chopped

½ cup chopped onion

½ cup whole cranberries

4 cups herb-flavored stuffing

In a large saucepan combine broth, pepper, celery, onions, and cranberries. Bring to a boil. Reduce heat, cover and cook for 5 minutes. Add stuffing. Toss with a fork. Makes 5 servings.

TO CUT THE ACIDITY LEVEL OF TOMATO-BASED SAUCES AND STEWS, SUCH AS CHILI OR SPAGHETTI SAUCE, ADD A PINCH OF BAKING SODA WHILE COOKING.

BASIC WHITE SAUCE

4 tablespoons butter

2 ½ tablespoons flour

½ teaspoon salt

¼ teaspoon pepper

2 cups milk

In a medium saucepan, melt butter. Stir in flour, salt, and pepper. Cook and stir over medium heat for 1 minute. Blend in milk, stirring constantly. Cook until mixture thickens. Use with vegetables and meat. Makes 2 cups.

• •

CHEESE SAUCE

8 ounces Cheddar cheese, grated

1 cup milk

1 teaspoon dry mustard

½ teaspoon basil

In a medium saucepan, combine all ingredients, mixing well. Cook and stir over low heat until sauce is smooth. Serve hot. Makes 2 cups.

SALT ADDED TO COOKING WATER WILL TOUGHEN CORN, SO SALT THE CORN AFTER IT'S COOKED.

GLAZED CARROTS ANYTIME

8 medium carrots

4 tablespoons apple juice

½ teaspoon cinnamon

⅛ teaspoon ground allspice

2 teaspoons grated orange peel

1¾ cups water

*2 teaspoons cornstarch mixed with
3 tablespoons water*

In a medium saucepan, combine carrots, apple juice, cinnamon, allspice, and orange peel. Cook and stir over medium heat until mixture begins to boil. Lower heat and simmer 20 minutes. Add cornstarch mixture, cook and stir until mixture thickens. Makes 4 servings.

Per Serving: Calories-95, Protein-2 gm, Fat-0 gm, Carbohydrates-23 gm, Cholesterol-0 mg, Sodium-76 mg.

ZESTY KERNEL CORN

*1 (16 ounce) package frozen
whole kernel corn*

½ cup salsa

¼ cup sliced ripe olives

Cook corn per package directions. Stir in salsa and olives. Heat. Makes 5 servings.

Per Serving: Calories-85, Protein-3 gm, Fat-1 gram, Carbohydrates-19 gm, Cholesterol-0 mg, Sodium-130 mg.

SKILLET FRIED CORN CAKES

½ cup yellow cornmeal

1 cup boiling water

3 tablespoons apple juice

1 cup whole kernel corn

2 egg whites

In a medium bowl, combine cornmeal, water, and apple juice. Mix well. Add corn. Beat egg whites until stiff peaks form. Fold into cornmeal mixture. Spray a large skillet with vegetable cooking spray. Drop cornmeal mixture by tablespoons into hot skillet. Brown on both sides. Makes 15 cakes.

Per Serving: Calories-34, Protein-1 gram, Fat-0.5 gm, Carbohydrates-7 gm, Cholesterol-0 mg, Sodium-33 mg.

NIPPY CUCUMBERS

2 medium cucumbers

1 tablespoon lime juice

1 teaspoon coarse salt

½ teaspoon chili powder

Super-Fast

Cut cucumbers lengthwise into quarters. Cut quarters into 2 inch pieces. Place in single layer on serving plate. Drizzle with lime juice. Sprinkle with salt and chili powder. Makes 30.

Per Serving (1 piece): Calories-2, Protein-0 gm, Fat-0 gm, Carbohydrates-1 gm, Cholesterol-0 mg, Sodium-75 mg.

CHEESE AND ZUCCHINI CASSEROLE

Vegetable cooking spray

4 medium zucchini, cut into ½ inch strips

½ teaspoon salt

4 ounces shredded Swiss cheese

½ cup plain low-fat yogurt

1 teaspoon minced onion

1 teaspoon Dijon mustard

Spray a 2 quart casserole with vegetable cooking spray. Set aside. In a large skillet, boil salted zucchini in 1 inch of water until tender. Drain zucchini and place in prepared casserole dish. In a small bowl, combine remaining cheese, yogurt, onion, and mustard. Mix well and spread over zucchini. Broil 4 to 5 minutes or until zucchini starts to brown. Makes 2 servings.

Per Serving: Calories-300, Protein-22 gm, Fat-7 gm, Carbohydrates-17 gm, Cholesterol-56 mg, Sodium-533 mg.

• •

VEGGIE CHEDDAR CHEESE SAUCE

½ cup evaporated skimmed milk

2 ounces sharp Cheddar cheese, shredded

⅛ teaspoon Worcestershire sauce

Super-Fast

In a small saucepan, heat milk to boiling. Remove from heat and add cheese and Worcestershire sauce. Cook and stir over low heat until cheese melts. Makes 2 servings.

Per Serving: Calories-165, Protein-129 gm, Fat-10 gm, Carbohydrates-8 gm, Cholesterol-32 mg, Sodium-317 mg.

CRISPY HASH BROWNS WITH ZUCCHINI

2 large potatoes, peeled and shredded

1 zucchini, peeled and shredded

1 onion, grated

2 egg whites

⅓ cup matza meal

1 tablespoon plus 1 teaspoon low-sodium soy sauce

In a large bowl, combine all ingredients. Mix well. Spray a large skillet with vegetable cooking spray. Add potato mixture. Cook over medium heat until brown and crusty. Turn once. Makes 4 servings.

Per Serving: Calories-66, Protein-4 gm, Fat-trace, Carbohydrates-9 gm, Cholesterol-0 mg, Sodium-217 mg.

• •

ONION HASH BROWNS

2 teaspoons butter

2 large potatoes, peeled and diced

1 small onion, chopped

Super-Fast

In a large skillet, melt butter. Add potatoes and onion, cover and cook over low heat for 10 minutes. Remove cover. Cook and stir over high heat until golden brown. Makes 4 servings.

Per Serving: Calories-137, Protein-3 gm, Fat-2 gm, Carbohydrates-27 gm, Cholesterol-5 mg, Sodium-28 mg.

FLAVOR OF FRENCH FRIED POTATOES

3 medium potatoes

Vegetable oil

1 teaspoon salt

½ teaspoon sugar

½ teaspoon paprika

¼ teaspoon dry mustard

⅛ teaspoon garlic powder

Cut potatoes lengthwise into eighths. Place potatoes, cut side down, on an ungreased 15 x 10 x ½ inch jelly roll pan. Brush lightly with vegetable oil. In a small bowl, mix salt, sugar, paprika, dry mustard, and garlic. Sprinkle half of mixture over potatoes. Broil 3 inches from heat for 8 minutes. Turn, brush potatoes with remaining mixture. Broil until golden brown. Makes 6 servings.

Per Serving: Calories-80, Protein-2 gm, Fat-2 gm, Carbohydrates-14 gm, Cholesterol-0 mg, Sodium-370 mg.

FOR FASTER BAKED POTATOES, SOAK THE POTATOES IN HOT, SALTY WATER FOR ABOUT A HALF-HOUR BEFORE BAKING.

POTATO CRISP PANCAKES

3 pounds potatoes, grated

4 egg whites, beaten

1 large onion, diced

¼ cup flour

1 tablespoon low-sodium soy sauce

Vegetable cooking spray

In a large bowl, combine potatoes, egg whites, and onion. Mix well. Add flour and soy sauce. Mix well. Spray a medium skillet with non-stick vegetable cooking spray. Drop mixture by spoonfuls into skillet. Flatten with spatula. Cook over high heat until crispy. Makes 16 pancakes.

Per Serving: Calories-107, Protein-6 gm, Fat-0 gm, Carbohydrates-20 gm, Cholesterol-0 mg, Sodium-37 mg.

• •

POTATO TOPPING

1 cup low-fat cottage cheese, drained

2 tablespoons low-fat buttermilk

¼ teaspoon fresh lemon juice

Combine all ingredients in a blender. Cover and blend until smooth.

Per Serving (1 tablespoon): Calories-11, Protein-1.8 gm, Fat-trace, Carbohydrates-.5 gm, Cholesterol-42 mg, Sodium-40 mg.

MARSHMALLOW SWEET POTATO BALLS

Vegetable cooking spray

1 (18 ounce) can sweet potatoes

1 tablespoon packed brown sugar

6 large marshmallows

1 tablespoon margarine, melted

⅓ cup cornflake crumbs

Preheat oven to 450°. Spray an 8 x 8 x 2 inch baking dish with vegetable cooking spray. Set aside. In a medium bowl, mash sweet potatoes and brown sugar. Shape ⅓ of the potato mixture around each marshmallow and form into a ball. Brush each sweet potato ball with margarine, then roll in cornflakes to coat. Place in prepared baking pan. Bake at 450° for 8 to 10 minutes or until coating is light brown. Makes 6 servings.

Per Serving: Calories-135, Protein-2 gm, Fat-2 gm, Carbohydrates-28 gm, Cholesterol-0 mg, Sodium-95 mg.

FOR SNOW WHITE, COOKED CAULIFLOWER AND POTATOES, COOK IN WATER THAT CONTAINS A TABLESPOON OF LEMON JUICE.

SCALLOP FETTUCCINI

1 red pepper, chopped
¼ cup sliced green onions
2 tablespoons reduced-calorie margarine
2 tablespoons lime juice
2 pounds sea scallops
2 cups cubed fresh pineapple
1 cup Chinese pea pod halves
Cooked fettuccini

In a 10 inch skillet, combine pepper, onions, margarine, and lime juice. Cook and stir over medium heat until margarine melts. Add scallops. Cook 12 minutes, stirring frequently, until scallops are white. Add pineapple and pea pods. Cook until all ingredients are hot. Remove scallop mixture, keeping warm. Boil liquid in skillet until slightly thick. Serve scallop mixture and sauce over fettuccine. Makes 6 servings.

Per Serving: Calories-355, Protein-39 gm, Fat-6 gm, Carbohydrates-34 gm, Cholesterol-80 mg, Sodium 430-mg.

INDIVIDUALLY WRAP TOMATOES IN NEWSPAPER TO RIPEN THEM AND KEEP THEM FRESH FOR WEEKS.

NOODLE CHEESE BAKE

Vegetable cooking spray

1 (16 ounce) package egg noodles

1 cup low-fat cottage cheese

¾ cup shredded low-fat Cheddar cheese

½ cup low-fat sour cream

⅓ cup chopped green onion

3 tablespoons grated Parmesan cheese

2 egg whites

1 egg

Preheat oven to 350°. Coat an 8 x 8 x 2 inch baking dish with vegetable cooking spray. Set aside. Cook noodles as directed on package. Drain. Return to saucepan. Combine noodles with cottage cheese, Cheddar cheese, sour cream, onion, Parmesan cheese, egg whites, and egg. Spread mixture in prepared baking dish. Bake at 350° uncovered for 30 minutes or until edges are golden brown. Let stand a few minutes before serving. Makes 6 servings.

Per Serving: Calories-275, Protein-22 gm, Fat-9 gm, Carbohydrates-25 gm, Cholesterol-80 mg, Sodium-690 mg.

CHICKEN PIZZA BREAD

1 loaf French bread

1 (8 ounce) can pizza sauce

2 cups cubed cooked chicken

1 (2¼ ounce) can sliced ripe olives, drained

1 cup shredded reduced-fat mozzarella cheese

Preheat oven to 425°. Split bread horizontally. Place bread, cut side up, on cookie sheet. Spread pizza sauce over bread. Top with chicken and olives. Sprinkle with cheese. Bake at 425° for 12 minutes or until cheese melts. Makes 6 servings.

Per Serving: Calories-305, Protein-22 gm, Fat-12 gm, Carbohydrates-29 gm, Cholesterol-60 mg, Sodium-660 mg.

• •

HAM AND CHEESE TURNOVERS

Vegetable cooking spray

1 cup part-skim ricotta cheese

4 ounces mozzarella cheese, shredded

4 ounces chopped ham

2 teaspoons oregano leaves

4 refrigerated buttermilk biscuits

Preheat oven to 400°. Coat a baking sheet with vegetable cooking spray. Set aside. In a large bowl, combine cheeses, ham, and oregano. Mix well. Roll each biscuit between 2 sheets of waxed paper, forming a 6 inch circle. Spoon ¼ of the mixture into center of each biscuit. Moisten edges of dough, then fold over mixture, turnover style. Using a fork, press edges to seal. Place turnovers on prepared baking sheet. Bake for 10 to 12 minutes, or until golden brown. Makes 4 servings.

Per Serving: Calories-299, Protein-22 gm, Fat-15 gm, Carbohydrates-17 gm, Cholesterol-66 mg, Sodium-686 mg.

HAM AND CHEESE BAGEL SANDWICHES

*2 pumpernickel bagels, split and
    toasted*

4 teaspoons honey mustard

4 (1 ounce) slices cooked honey ham

4 (½ ounce) slices Swiss cheese

Super-Fast

Preheat oven to 400°. Spread each bagel half with 1 teaspoon mustard. Place bagel on cookie sheet. Top each bagel with one slice ham and one slice cheese. Bake for 3 to 5 minutes or until cheese melts. Makes
4 servings.

Per Serving (half bagel): Calories-185, Protein-13 gm, Fat-7 gm, Carbohydrates-18 gm, Cholesterol-30 mg, Sodium-620 mg.

GROUND BEEF SLOPPY JOES

1 pound extra lean ground beef

1 onion, chopped

1 (10¾ ounce) can reduced-fat tomato soup

2 teaspoons Worcestershire sauce

3 drops red pepper sauce

6 hamburger buns

In a medium skillet, cook ground beef and onion over medium heat until beef is brown. Drain on paper towels. Return to skillet. Add soup, Worcestershire sauce, and pepper sauce. Cook until hot. Stir occasionally. Fill buns with mixture. Makes 6 servings.

Per Serving: Calories-240, Protein-22 gm, Fat-4 gm, Carbohydrates-31 gm, Cholesterol-50 mg, Sodium-482 mg.

MINI FRUIT TACOS

1 cup sour cream

2 tablespoons sugar

1 tablespoon fresh lime juice

2 teaspoons grated lime peel

24 mini taco shells

Vegetable cooking spray

2 tablespoons sugar

4 cups chopped, assorted fruit

In a small bowl, combine sour cream, sugar, lime juice, and lime peel. Mix well. Cover. Chill for 30 minutes. Preheat oven to 350°. Place taco shells on ungreased cookie sheet. Spray outside of shells with vegetable cooking spray. Sprinkle each with ¼ teaspoon sugar. Bake at 350° for 5 minutes or until lightly browned. Cool. Spoon 2 tablespoons chopped fruit into each shell. Top with lime cream. Makes 12 servings.

Per Serving (2 tacos): Calories-50, Protein-1 gram, Fat-2 gm, Carbohydrates-8 gm, Cholesterol-5 mg, Sodium-30 mg.

Let the Good Times Roll

(Breads, Biscuits, and Rolls)

SOUR CREAM COFFEE CAKE

1 cup sugar

2 eggs

1 cup sour cream

1 teaspoon vanilla extract

1 stick butter, melted

1½ teaspoons baking powder

1½ cups flour

Preheat oven to 350°. In a medium bowl, combine sugar, eggs, sour cream, and vanilla. Add melted butter. Combine dry ingredients and add to liquid ingredients, mixing well. Pour batter into a 9 inch square baking pan. Spoon topping over batter. Bake at 350° for 45 minutes.

Topping:

¼ cup sugar

¼ cup packed brown sugar

¼ cup chopped walnuts

In a small bowl, combine all ingredients and spoon over batter.

TO KEEP ROLLS WARM LONGER, PLACE A PIECE OF ALUMINUM FOIL UNDER A CLOTH NAPKIN IN THE BOTTOM OF THE SERVING BASKET.

PRIZE WINNING COFFEE CAKE

¾ cup sugar

¼ cup soft shortening

1 egg

½ cup milk

1½ cups flour

2 teaspoons baking powder

½ teaspoon salt

½ cup packed brown sugar

½ teaspoon cinnamon

Preheat oven to 375°. In a medium bowl, combine sugar, shortening, and egg. Add milk. In a separate bowl, sift flour, baking powder, and salt. Add to liquid mixture and mix well. Pour batter into a greased and floured 8 inch square baking pan. Sprinkle brown sugar and cinnamon over batter. Bake at 375° for 30 minutes.

COFFEE CAKE CRUMB TOPPING

2 tablespoons butter

2 tablespoons sugar

¼ cup flour, sifted

¼ cup dry bread crumbs

½ teaspoon cinnamon

In a medium bowl, combine all ingredients. Mix to consistency of coarse crumbs. Sprinkle over coffee cake before baking.

COFFEE CAKE ICING

Super-Fast

1 cup confectioners' sugar

2 tablespoons warm milk

½ teaspoon vanilla

In a small bowl, combine all ingredients, mixing until smooth. Frosting for 1 (12 inch) coffee cake.

● ●

DELICIOUS BLUEBERRY MUFFINS

2 tablespoons shortening

2 tablespoons sugar

1 egg

2 cups flour

3 tablespoons baking powder

¼ teaspoon salt

1 cup milk

1¼ cups floured blueberries

Preheat oven to 400°. In a medium bowl, cream shortening, and sugar. Add egg, flour, baking powder, salt, and milk. Mix well. Fold in blueberries. Pour into greased muffin tins, $^2/_3$ full. Bake at 400° for 20 to 25 minutes.

TO KEEP BUGS OUT OF YOUR FLOUR, PLACE AN UNWRAPPED STICK OF SPEARMINT GUM IN THE FLOUR BIN.

STICKY BUN'S FOR A BREAK

⅓ cup butter or margarine, melted

⅓ cup packed brown sugar

⅓ cup chopped pecans

2¼ cups Bisqick® mix

⅔ cup milk

2 tablespoons sugar

Preheat oven to 425 degrees. In a small bowl, combine butter, brown sugar, and pecans. Mix well. Spray muffin cups with cooking spray. Pour mixture evenly among cups. In medium bowl, combine Bisquick, milk, and sugar. Mix well. Place a spoonful of dough in each muffin cup. Bake 10 to 15 minutes. Turn pan upside down onto cookie sheet for a few minutes to allow mixture to drizzle over buns.

PAT'S QUICK DOUGHNUTS

1 (10 count) can refrigerated biscuits

2 cups vegetable oil

1½ tablespoons butter, melted

3 tablespoons sugar

2 teaspoons cinnamon

Super-Fast

To make doughnuts, cut the center out of each biscuit. Heat oil in a deep skillet until hot. Drop doughnuts into hot oil and cook until lightly brown. Turn and brown on second side. Drain on paper towels. Brush doughnuts with melted butter. On a plate, mix sugar and cinnamon. Roll doughnuts in sugar mixture.

ROLL AND EAT TORTILLA TREATS

4 flour tortillas

¼ cup butter, melted

¼ cup cinnamon

¼ cup sugar

Brush one side of tortilla with melted butter. Sprinkle with cinnamon and sugar. Roll. Place seam side down on microwave safe plate. Microwave on high for 30 seconds.

• •

BANANA NUT BREAD

½ cup butter

1 cup sugar

2 eggs

4 bananas, mashed

2 cups flour

1 teaspoon baking soda

½ teaspoon salt

1 cup chopped nuts

Preheat oven to 350°. In a large bowl, cream butter and sugar. Add eggs and bananas. Sift flour, soda, and salt. Add to banana mixture. Add nuts and mix well. Pour into a greased 8½ x 4½ inch loaf pan. Bake at 350° for 45 to 50 minutes.

TO GET RID OF THE HICCUPS, TRY EATING A SPOONFUL OF PEANUT BUTTER.

QUICK FIX BANANA BREAD

1½ cups mashed bananas

½ teaspoon vanilla extract

3 eggs

2⅓ cups Bisquick®

1 cup sugar

⅓ cup vegetable oil

Preheat oven to 350°. In a large bowl, combine bananas, vanilla, eggs, Bisquick®, sugar, and oil. Mix well. Pour into a greased 9 x 5 x 3 inch loaf pan. Bake for 55 minutes to 1 hour. Cool before serving.

ORANGE ALMOND BREAD

2 tablespoon solid shortening

¼ cup sugar

1 egg

2 cups cake flour

1 tablespoon baking powder

1 teaspoon salt

1 cup orange juice

1 teaspoon grated orange rind

1 cup sliced blanched almonds

Preheat oven to 350°. In a large bowl, cream shortening, sugar, and egg. Set aside. In a medium bowl, sift flour, baking powder, and salt. Add to creamed mixture, mixing well. Add orange juice and orange rind. Blend thoroughly. Add nuts. Pour into greased and floured 9 x 5 x 3 inch loaf pan. Bake at 350° for 1 hour.

PECAN NUT BREAD

3 cups flour

4 teaspoons baking powder

1 teaspoon salt

¾ cup sugar

1 cup chopped pecans

1 egg, beaten

1½ cups milk

2 tablespoons shortening, melted

Preheat oven to 350°. In a large bowl, sift flour, baking powder, salt, and sugar. Add nuts. Set aside. In a medium bowl, combine egg, milk, and shortening. Add to dry mixture, stirring until all ingredients are combined. Pour into a greased and floured 9 x 5 x 3 inch loaf pan. Bake at 350° for 55 minutes.

• •

PUMPKIN BREAD

3 cups flour

1 teaspoon baking soda

1 teaspoon salt

1 tablespoon cinnamon

1 tablespoon nutmeg

2 cups sugar

2 cups canned pumpkin

4 eggs, beaten

1¼ cup vegetable oil

Preheat oven to 350°. In a large bowl, combine flour, soda, salt, cinnamon, nutmeg, and sugar. Set aside. In a medium bowl, combine pumpkin, eggs, and oil. Add to dry mixture.

Mix well. Dough will be very stiff. Place batter into two greased and floured 9 x 5 x 3 inch loaf pans. Bake at 350° for 1 hour. Test bread for doneness, after 45 minutes by inserting a toothpick into center of loaf. If toothpick comes out clean, bread is done. Makes 2 loaves.

FRIED GARLIC BREAD

1 loaf French bread, thinly sliced

2 cloves garlic, minced

½ stick butter

¼ cup grated Parmesan cheese

Rub bread slices with garlic. Melt butter in a large skillet and brown bread on each side. Sprinkle with Parmesan cheese before serving.

CHEESY FRENCH BREAD

¼ cup fresh chives

1 cup Dijon mustard

1 pound Swiss cheese, shredded

2 cloves garlic, minced

1 loaf French bread

In a medium bowl, combine chives, mustard, cheese, and garlic. Mix well. Slice bread into ¼ inch pieces. Spread each slice with cheese mixture. Place bread on cookie sheet and broil until cheese melts.

TURN THE STACK OF COFFEE FILTERS INSIDE OUT AND THEY ARE EASY TO SEPARATE.

TOASTED BREADSTICKS

4 slices bread

2 tablespoons butter or margarine

¼ teaspoon garlic salt

2 tablespoons grated Parmesan cheese

Super-Fast

Preheat oven to 350°. Spread bread with margarine. Sprinkle with garlic salt and cheese. Cut each slice into 4 strips, place on ungreased cookie sheet. Bake at 350° for 15 minutes. Makes 16 sticks.

DRESSED UP BROWN N SERVE ROLLS

*1 (12 count) package brown
 and serve rolls*

2½ tablespoons butter, melted

⅛ teaspoon onion salt

½ teaspoon poppy seeds

Super-Fast

Preheat oven to 400°. Place rolls on ungreased cookie sheet. Brush tops with butter. Sprinkle with onion salt and poppy seeds. Bake at 400° for 10 minutes. Makes 1 dozen.

CORNMEAL MIXED WITH LEMON JUICE MAKES A GREAT MASSAGE FOR THE FACE, CLEANING THE PORES AND REFRESHING THE SKIN.

CHOCOLATE NUT ROLLS

⅓ cup chocolate flavored syrup

2 tablespoons butter, melted

½ cup chopped walnuts

1 (8 count) package refrigerated breadsticks

Preheat oven to 350°. In a 9 inch round cake pan, combine syrup and butter. Sprinkle nuts over syrup mixture. Separate, but do not uncoil, breadsticks. Arrange dough coils over nuts. Bake at 350° for 20 to 25 minutes, or until golden brown. Let stand 2 or 3 minutes before serving. Serve warm.

• •

MELT IN YOUR MOUTH BISCUITS

6 tablespoons butter, softened

2 cups flour

¾ cup half and half

2 teaspoons baking powder

½ teaspoon salt

Preheat oven to 400°. In food processor, combine butter, flour, half and half, baking powder, and salt. Mix well. Place dough on floured board, knead 10 to 12 strokes. Roll to ½ inch thickness. Cut dough with floured biscuit cutter. Place biscuits on greased cookie sheet. Bake at 400° for 10 minutes or until just brown.

BISCUITS WITH A BITE

Super-Fast

1 (10 count) tube refrigerated biscuits

3 tablespoons butter, melted

½ teaspoon chili powder

½ cup shredded Cheddar cheese

¼ cup chopped jalapeno peppers

Preheat oven to 350°. Cut biscuits into quarters. Set aside. In a small bowl, mix butter and chili powder. Pour into a 9 inch pie plate. Place biscuit pieces in pan and toss to coat. Sprinkle cheese and peppers on top. Bake at 350° for 15 minutes or until brown.

• •

PERK IT UP DROP BISCUITS

2 cups original Bisquick   mix

¼ cup margarine, softened

2 tablespoons sugar

⅔ cup milk

¼ cup peach preserves

Preheat oven to 450 °. In large bowl, combine Bisquick, margarine, sugar, and milk. Beat well. Drop by tablespoon onto greased cookie sheet, 2 inches apart. Make a shallow well in center of each with the back of spoon dipped in water. Fill each with 1 teaspoon of preserves. Bake 10 to 15 minutes or until golden brown.

MOM'S BUTTERMILK BISCUITS

2 cups flour

1 teaspoon salt

½ teaspoon baking soda

1½ teaspoons baking powder

4 tablespoons solid shortening

1 cup buttermilk

Preheat oven to 450°. Sift flour, salt, baking soda, and baking powder. Cut in shortening until mixture resembles coarse crumbs. Make a well in the dough, add milk and combine with a fork until dough sticks to fork. On a floured board, knead dough 10 to 12 strokes. Roll to ½ inch thickness. Cut with a biscuit cutter or small glass. Place biscuits on greased cookie sheet. Bake at 450° for 12 to15 minutes.

● ●

SWEET POTATO BISCUITS

1½ cups flour

2 tablespoons baking powder

¾ teaspoon salt

½ cup solid shortening

1 cup milk

1½ cups mashed sweet potatoes

Preheat oven to 425°. Sift flour, baking powder, and salt. Cut in shortening until mixture resembles coarse crumbs. Set aside. In a small bowl, combine milk and sweet potatoes. Add to dry mixture, mixing well. Place dough on a floured surface, and knead 10 to 12 strokes. Roll dough to ½ inch thickness. Cut with floured biscuit cutter or small glass. Place biscuits on greased cookie sheet. Bake at 425° for 12 to 15 minutes.

CAMPING FRIED BISCUITS

2 cups flour

3¾ teaspoons baking powder

1 teaspoon salt

6 tablespoons solid shortening

¾ cup milk

Sift flour, baking powder, and salt. Cut in shortening until mixture resembles coarse crumbs. Make a well in the dough, adding milk all at once. Stir with a fork until dough sticks to fork. Knead 10 to 12 strokes. Place dough on lightly floured board. Roll dough to ¼ inch thickness and cut with 2½ inch cookie cutter. Cook in lightly greased, hot skillet over low heat until biscuits are brown on underside and raised to 1 inch thickness. Turn and brown on other side.

CRISPY BACON CHEESE BISCUITS

⅔ cup milk

2 cups Bisquick®

¼ cup shredded Cheddar cheese

4 slices bacon, cooked crisp and crumbled

Preheat oven to 450°. In a medium bowl, mix milk and Bisquick® until smooth. Add cheese and bacon. Mix well. Drop by teaspoon onto ungreased baking sheet. Bake at 450° for 10 to 15 minutes.

PRESS A CHEESE BISCUITS

1 stick butter, softened

1 cup flour

¼ teaspoon cayenne pepper

½ cup chopped nuts

½ teaspoon caraway seeds

1 cup shredded sharp Cheddar cheese

Preheat oven to 325°. In a medium bowl, combine butter, flour, pepper, nuts, caraway seeds, and cheese. Mix well. Pinch off dough and roll into small balls. Place on a lightly greased baking sheet. Press with a fork to flatten. Bake at 325° for 10 to 12 minutes.

BISCUIT CHEESE DROPS

Super-Fast

2 cups Bisquick®

1 cup grated Cheddar cheese

⅛ teaspoon salt

1 cup milk

Preheat oven to 450°. In a medium bowl, combine Bisquick®, cheese, and salt. Add milk. Drop by tablespoons onto a lightly greased baking sheet. Bake at 450° for 15 minutes or until golden brown.

RUB AN EGG WHITE ON CHEWING GUM TO REMOVE IT FROM ANY SURFACE, INCLUDING YOUR HAIR.

PULL APART CINNAMON BISCUITS

Super-Fast

4 (7.5 ounce) cans refrigerated biscuits

1½ cups packed brown sugar

¾ cup butter

2¼ teaspoons cinnamon

Preheat oven to 350°. Quarter biscuits and place in a well greased bundt pan. In a small saucepan, bring brown sugar, butter, and cinnamon to a boil. Pour over biscuits. Bake at 350° for 25 to 30 minutes.

• •

BISCUITS FROM SCRATCH

3 cups flour

2 tablespoons baking powder

¾ teaspoon salt

1 cup heavy cream

Preheat oven to 425°. Sift flour, baking powder, and salt into a medium bowl. Add cream, stirring just enough to dampen all the flour. Place dough on a lightly floured board and knead 10 to12 strokes. Roll dough to a ½ inch thickness. Cut with floured biscuit cutter. Place biscuits on a greased baking sheet. Bake at 425° for 12 to 15 minutes.

BREAKFAST CINNAMON BISCUITS

2 (10 count) cans refrigerated biscuits

⅓ cup butter, melted

⅓ cup packed brown sugar

¼ cup sugar

1 teaspoon cinnamon

⅓ cup chopped pecans

Preheat oven to 350°. Using a 9 inch round cake pan, over-lap biscuits in a spiral fashion. In a small bowl, combine butter, brown sugar, sugar, cinnamon, and nuts. Pour over biscuits. Bake at 350° for 30 minutes.

DICED HAM CORNBREAD

Super-Fast

1 cup cooked ham, diced

2 cups self-rising cornmeal

1½ cups milk

2 eggs

Preheat oven to 400°. In a medium bowl, combine ham, cornmeal, milk, and eggs. Mix well. Pour into a greased 9 inch baking pan. Bake at 400° for 35 minutes.

FOR QUICK BREAD CRUMBS, PLACE TWO PIECES OF TOAST IN A SANDWICH BAG AND CRUSH WITH A ROLLING PIN.

CREAM STYLE CORNBREAD

1 cup self-rising cornmeal

½ teaspoon sugar

3 eggs

1 cup cream style corn

1 cup sour cream

Preheat oven to 400°. In a medium bowl, combine cornmeal, sugar, eggs, corn, and sour cream. Mix well. Pour into a greased 8 x 8 x 2 inch baking pan. Bake at 400° for 35 minutes.

• •

JALAPENO CORNBREAD

1 egg

1¼ cups milk

3 tablespoons butter, melted

1½ cups self-rising cornmeal

½ cup shredded Cheddar cheese

3 tablespoons finely chopped jalapeno pepper

Preheat oven to 400°. In a medium bowl, combine egg, milk, and butter. Add cornmeal, cheese, and pepper. Mix well. Pour into a greased 9 inch baking pan. Bake at 400° for 25 to 30 minutes.

KEEP ANTS OUT OF YOUR KITCHEN BY PLACING CUCUMBER PEELS ON THE WINDOWSILL.

SOUTHERN HUSHPUPPIES

2 cups cornmeal

2 teaspoons baking powder

1 teaspoon salt

⅓ cup diced onion

⅔ cup milk

1 egg

2 cups vegetable oil

In a medium bowl, combine cornmeal, baking powder, salt, onion, milk, and egg. Shape into balls and fry in hot oil until golden brown. Drain on paper towels. Serve hot.

• •

1800'S CORNBREAD PATTIES

1 cup cornmeal

¼ cup flour

1 teaspoon salt

⅛ teaspoon baking soda

1½ cups boiling water

⅓ cup vegetable oil

In a medium bowl, combine cornmeal, flour, salt, and baking soda. Mix well. Pour boiling water over mixture and stir until moistened. Let cool. Shape into small patties and fry in hot oil.

SKILLET FRIED CORNBREAD

1 cup cornmeal

½ teaspoon baking soda

½ teaspoon salt

2 eggs, beaten

1¼ cups buttermilk

2 tablespoons shortening

In a medium bowl, combine cornmeal, soda, and salt. Add eggs and buttermilk. Mix until smooth. In a medium skillet, heat shortening until hot. Drop batter by tablespoons into hot oil. Brown on each side. Drain on paper towels.

● ●

RUFFIN-IT CORNBREAD

1½ cups white cornmeal

½ teaspoon salt

¾ cup boiling water

⅓ cup vegetable oil

Super-Fast

In a medium bowl, combine cornmeal and salt. Pour boiling water over mixture, stirring constantly. In a medium skillet, heat oil until very hot. Drop batter by tablespoons, cooking on both sides until light brown. Drain on paper towels.

FOR EXTRA CRISPY FRENCH TOAST, USE LIGHTLY TOASTED BREAD THAT HAS BEEN DIPPED IN EGG BATTER.

OLD TIME CRACKLING BREAD

1½ cups white cornmeal

3 cups boiling water

¼ teaspoon salt

1 cup crushed cracklings

Oil

In a large bowl, combine cornmeal, water, and salt. Add cracklings, mixing well. Form into cakes. Fry with a little oil until brown on both sides.

• •

PLANTATION SPOONBREAD

1 cup cornmeal

3 cups milk, divided

3 eggs, beaten

1 teaspoon salt

1 tablespoon baking powder

2 tablespoons butter or margarine, melted

Preheat oven to 350°. In a large saucepan, stir cornmeal into 2 cups of the milk. Bring to a boil, making a mush. Add 1 cup of the milk, and eggs. Stir in salt, baking powder, and butter. Bake at 350° for 30 minutes.

SIZZLING HOT WAFFLES

2 cups flour

1 tablespoon baking powder

½ teaspoon salt

3 eggs, separated

1½ cups milk

5 tablespoons shortening, melted

In a large bowl, combine flour, baking powder, and salt. In a small bowl, beat egg yolks, milk, and shortening. Add to dry ingredients. Beat egg whites and fold into batter. Pour into hot waffle iron and cook until brown.

BUTTERMILK PANCAKES

1 egg, beaten

1¼ cups buttermilk

½ teaspoon baking soda

1¼ cups flour

1 teaspoon sugar

1 teaspoon baking powder

½ teaspoon salt

Oil

In a medium bowl, combine all ingredients, beating until smooth. Pour ½ cup batter on a hot griddle that has been coated with a small amount of oil. Turn pancakes when bubbles form in batter.

TO MAKE LIGHT, FLUFFY WAFFLES, USE BUTTERMILK WITH A PINCH OF BAKING SODA, RATHER THAN WHOLE MILK.

HOT-N-RIZIN ROLLS

1 (¼ ounce) package dry yeast

2 cups warm water

¾ cup butter, melted

¼ cup sugar

1 egg, beaten

4 cups self-rising flour

In a large bowl, combine yeast and warm water. Add melted butter. Gradually add sugar, stirring constantly. Add beaten egg, then flour. Stir until ingredients are thoroughly mixed. Let stand 20 minutes. Preheat oven to 400°. Drop dough by spoonfuls into greased muffin tins. Bake at 400° for 20 minutes. Makes 2 dozen.

• •

HOME STYLE BREAD

(Bread Machine Recipe)

¾ cup milk

¼ cup water

4 teaspoons margarine or butter

3 cups bread flour

4 teaspoons sugar

¾ teaspoon salt

¼ teaspoon baking soda

1 teaspoon active dry yeast

Select directions for 1½ pound loaf. Add ingredients according to manufacturer's directions. Select Basic White Bread cycle. Makes 16 slices.

SPICY NACHO BREADSTICKS

1 cup finely crushed spicy nacho flavored
  tortilla chips

1 (11 ounce) can refrigerated breadsticks

Preheat oven to 375 degrees. In shallow dish or pan, add tortilla chips. Separate dough into strips. Press dough into chips on both sides. Place on large cookie sheet. Bake 10 to 15 minutes or until golden brown. Makes 12 breadsticks.

• •

MAKE IT SPECIAL BREAD

1 tablespoon butter

½ cup chopped green onions

1 garlic clove, minced

1 (11 ounce) can refrigerated crusty French loaf

Preheat oven to 350 degrees. In small skillet, melt butter over medium heat. Add onions and garlic. Cook 3 minutes. Unroll dough, spread mixture on top, fold dough, place seam down on cooking sprayed cookie sheet. Bake 25 to 30 minutes or until golden brown.

QUICK AND EASY CRUSTY BREAD

2 tablespoons granular yeast

2 cups warm water

2 tablespoons sugar

1 tablespoon salt

¼ cup vegetable oil

6 to 6½ cups flour

In a large bowl, combine yeast and water. Add sugar, salt, oil, and 3 cups of the flour. Mix until smooth. Add remaining flour and knead for 10 minutes. Turn into greased bowl and let rise 45 minutes. Punch down and put dough into 8½ x 4½ x 2½ loaf pans. Bake at 375° for 30 minutes

• •

THANKSGIVING SAGE BREAD

(Bread Machine Recipe)

⅓ cup finely chopped onion

4 teaspoons margarine or butter

3 tablespoons water

3 cups bread flour

2 teaspoons sugar

2 teaspoons dried sage, crushed

¾ teaspoon salt

1 teaspoon active dry yeast

Select directions for 1½ pound loaf. In a small saucepan, cook onion in hot margarine. Cool slightly. Add onion mixture and remaining ingredients to the bread machine, according to manufacturer's directions. Select Basic White Bread cycle. Great for turkey sandwiches.

ADD A TOUCH OF CHEESE BREAD

1 loaf French bread
¼ cup butter or margarine
1 cup shredded cheddar cheese
¼ cup grated parmesan cheese

Preheat oven to 400 degrees. Cut bread in half, place on cookie sheet. Spread butter on both sides. Top with cheddar cheese and parmesan cheese. Bake 5 to 10 minutes.

• •

GLAZE FOR HOMEMADE BREAD

1 egg yolk
2 tablespoons sugar
3 tablespoons milk

In a small bowl, combine all ingredients, mixing well. Brush over bread dough before baking.

BUTTERED BREAD CRUMBS

Super-Fast

4 tablespoons butter

1 cup fresh bread crumbs

In a medium skillet, melt butter and add bread crumbs. Cook and stir until crumbs are lightly toasted and butter is absorbed. An excellent topping for casseroles.

HERB SPREAD FOR BREAD

⅓ cup margarine or butter, softened

2 tablespoons grated Parmesan cheese

¼ teaspoon dried basil

¼ teaspoon dried oregano

In a small bowl, combine all ingredients, mixing well. Keep refrigerated until ready to use.

ONION SPREAD

⅓ cup margarine or butter, softened

2 tablespoons finely chopped onion

⅛ teaspoon cayenne pepper

In a small bowl, combine all ingredients. Mix well. Keep refrigerated until ready to use.

REMOVE ODORS FROM YOUR REFRIGERATOR BY PLACING A PEELED RAW POTATO INSIDE.

GARLIC SPREAD

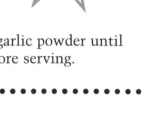

⅓ cup butter or margarine,
   softened

¼ teaspoon garlic powder

In a small bowl, combine butter and garlic powder until
well mixed. Let stand 30 minutes before serving.

• •

PIMIENTO CHEESE SPREAD

1 (16 ounce) package Cheddar cheese, grated

¾ cup mayonnaise

1 (2 ounce) jar chopped pimientos

¼ teaspoon Tabasco® sauce

½ teaspoon salt

In a small bowl, combine all ingredients, mixing well.
Serve immediately.

• •

STRAWBERRY JAM

3 cups large, firm strawberries

3 cups sugar

Wash strawberries and hull. In a large saucepan, crush berries and cook and stir until pulp begins to boil. Add sugar
and continue to cook and stir until mixture thickens. Pour
into sterile jars and seal. Makes 3 (6 ounce) jars.

PLUM JAM

1 pound plums

1 cup water

¾ pound sugar

Water

Clean plums. Place in a large saucepan and cover with water. Cook for 10 to 15 minutes or until skins are tender. Cool and remove stones. Add sugar, cooking on low until sugar is dissolved. Turn up heat and cook rapidly until mixture is thick. Pour into sterile jar and seal. Makes ½ pint.

• •

RHUBARB JAM

2½ pounds rhubarb

1½ pounds sugar

½ cup water

Rind of 2 oranges

Juice of 2 oranges

Wash rhubarb and cut into small pieces. In a large saucepan, combine rhubarb, sugar, and water. Add orange rind and orange juice. Cook over low heat for 35 minutes, stirring occasionally. Pour into sterile jars and seal. Makes 6 (6 ounce) jars.

EASILY CUT RHUBARB INTO PIECES BY USING SHEARS, RATHER THAN A KNIFE.

PEACH PRESERVES

2 pounds peaches

3 cups sugar

2 cups water

Remove skin from peaches. Cut peaches in half and remove stones. In a large saucepan, boil sugar and water until syrup coats a spoon. Add peaches and boil until syrup is thick. Mash. Pour into sterile jars and seal. Makes 3½ pints.

• •

PEAR AND APPLE JAM

1 pint pears, diced

1 pint apples, diced

Rind of 1 lemon

Juice of 1 lemon

3½ cups sugar

In a large saucepan, combine all ingredients. Cook on low heat until sugar is dissolved. Bring to a rapid boil and cook until mixture is thick and clear. Cool slightly. Pour into sterile jars and seal. Makes 1½ pints.

PULL-APART CINNAMON ROLLS

Vegetable cooking spray

3 (11 ounce) packages soft
    breadsticks

¾ cup fat free squeeze margarine

1¼ cups sugar

2 heaping tablespoons cinnamon

Preheat oven to 325°. Coat a bundt pan with vegetable
cooking spray. Remove breadsticks from can. Cut each
stick in half. You will have 48 sticks. Roll each into a ball.
Set aside. Place margarine in a small bowl. In another bowl,
combine sugar and cinnamon. Roll balls in margarine, then
in sugar mixture. Place balls in prepared bundt pan. Bake at
325° for 40 to 45 minutes. Serve warm.

Per Serving: Calories-231, Protein-5 gm, Fat-3.8 gm, Carbohy-
drates-44 gm, Cholesterol-0 mg, Sodium-529 mg.

GINGERBREAD BANANA MUFFINS

1 box gingerbread mix

1 cup mashed bananas
    (use overly ripe bananas)

¾ cup quick-cooking oats

¾ cup water

2 egg whites

Preheat oven to 375°. Grease bottom of muffin tins. Set
aside. In a large bowl, combine all ingredients. Mix well.
Divide batter evenly in muffin cups. Bake at 375° for 15
to 20 minutes. Remove from pan immediately. Makes 16
muffins.

Per Serving (1 muffin): Calories-135, Protein-2 gm, Fat-3 gm, Car-
bohydrates-26 gm, Cholesterol-0 mg, Sodium-180 mg.

WHOLE WHEAT POPOVERS

Vegetable cooking spray

¾ cup all-purpose flour

¼ cup whole wheat flour

1 cup skim milk

¼ teaspoon salt

2 eggs

Preheat oven to 450°. Spray six 6-ounce custard cups with vegetable cooking spray. In a medium bowl, combine all ingredients. Mix well. Fill cups half full. Bake at 450° for 20 minutes. Serve hot. Makes 6 popovers.

Per Serving: Calories-115, Protein-6 gm, Fat-2 gm, Carbohydrates-18 gm, Cholesterol-70 mg, Sodium-140 mg.

• •

CLASSIC WHITE BREAD

(Bread Machine)

1 cup milk

¼ cup water

4 teaspoons margarine or butter

3 cups bread flour

4 teaspoons sugar

¾ teaspoon salt

1 teaspoon active dry yeast

Select directions for 1½ pound loaf. Add ingredients as directed by manufacturer. Makes 16 slices.

Per Serving (1 slice): Calories-114, Protein-4 gm, Fat-2 gm, Carbohydrates-21 gm, Cholesterol-1 mg, Sodium-119 mg.

CADILLAC WALNUT BREAD

(Bread Machine)

⅔ *cup milk*

1 egg

3 tablespoons water

2 tablespoons vegetable oil

3 cups bread flour

2 tablespoons sugar

¾ *teaspoon salt*

1 teaspoon active dry yeast

⅔ *cup chopped black walnuts*

Select directions for a 1½ pound loaf. Machine pan must have the capacity for 10 cups or more for this recipe. Add ingredients in the order directed by manufacturer. Select Basic White Bread cycle. Makes 16 slices.

Per Serving: Calories-156, Protein-5 gm, Fat-6 gm, Carbohydrates-21 gm, Cholesterol-14 mg, Sodium-110 mg.

IS IT A COOKED EGG OR A RAW EGG? PLACE EGG ON FLAT SURFACE AND SPIN IT. IF IT SPINS, THE EGG IS COOKED; AN UNCOOKED EGG WILL NOT SPIN.

ALL AMERICAN CORNBREAD

(Bread Machine)

1 cup water

2 teaspoons cooking oil

2¾ cups bread flour

½ cup yellow cornmeal

¼ cup grated Parmesan cheese

2 teaspoons sugar

¾ teaspoon salt

¾ teaspoon crushed dried basil

1 teaspoon active dry yeast

Select directions for 1½ pound loaf. Add ingredients in the order directed by manufacturer. Select Basic White Bread cycle. Makes 16 slices.

Per Serving: Calories-114, Protein-4 gm, Fat-2 gm, Carbohydrates-21 gm, Cholesterol-1 mg, Sodium-131 mg.

Sweet Sensations

(Pies, Cakes, Cookies, Desserts and Candy)

RANCHER'S FRUIT PIE

1½ cup sugar

1 cup crushed pineapple, undrained

3 eggs, lightly beaten

3 teaspoons flour

1 cup flaked coconut

6 tablespoons butter or margarine

1 (9 inch) unbaked piecrust

Preheat oven to 350°. In medium bowl, combine sugar, pineapple, eggs flour and coconut. Melt butter and add to other ingredients. Pour filling into pie shell. Bake one hour or until filling is set and browned.

• •

FRESH STRAWBERRY PIE

4 tablespoons strawberry flavored gelatin

1 cup sugar

4 tablespoons cornstarch

1 cup boiling water

1 quart fresh strawberries

1 (9 inch) baked piecrust

Whipped topping or whipped cream

In a medium saucepan, combine gelatin, sugar, cornstarch, and boiling water. Cook and stir over medium heat until mixture is thick and clear. Cool. Fold in strawberries. Pour mixture into baked piecrust. Garnish with whipped topping or whipped cream.

BLUEBERRY CREAM CHEESE PIE

1 (3 ounce) package cream cheese, softened

½ pint whipping cream

½ cup confectioners' sugar

1 (9 inch) crumb piecrust

1 (22 ounce) can blueberry pie filling

In a medium bowl, combine soft cream cheese and whipping cream. Using an electric mixer on high speed, beat until mixture is stiff. Add confectioners' sugar. Beat until well combined. Pour into piecrust. Top with blueberry pie filling. Chill before serving.

•••

OUT OF TIME PINK LEMONADE PIE

1 (8 ounce) package cream cheese

1 (15 ounce) can Eagle Brand® milk

1 (6 ounce) can pink lemonade

1 (8 ounce) carton frozen whipped topping

1 (9 inch) graham cracker crust

In blender, combine cream cheese, milk, lemonade, and whipped topping. Cover. Blend well. Pour into crust. Chill.

DIVINE ICE CREAM PIE

Super-Fast

1½ cups butter pecan ice cream,
   softened

1 (9 inch) graham cracker piecrust

2 (1⅓ ounce) English toffee flavored candy bars,
   crushed

1½ cups vanilla ice cream, softened

Spread butter pecan ice cream in bottom of piecrust.
Sprinkle half the candy bar mixture over ice cream. Freeze.
Spread vanilla ice cream over top of pie. Sprinkle with
remaining candy bar mixture. Freeze until firm.

CHOCOLATE BAR PIE

¼ cup milk

1½ cups miniature marshmallows

1 (7 ounce) milk chocolate bar, broken into
   pieces

1 cup whipping cream, cold

1 (9 inch) crumb piecrust

In a medium microwave-safe bowl, combine milk and
marshmallows. Microwave on high until marshmallows
melt. Stir often. Add chocolate pieces, stirring until chocolate melts and mixture is smooth. Cool. In a small bowl,
beat whipping cream until stiff peaks form. Fold into
chocolate mixture. Pour into piecrust. Cover and chill until
firm.

*TAKE AWAY SOME OF THE SUGARY SWEET TASTE
IN PECAN PIES BY ADDING A TEASPOON OF
VINEGAR TO THE BATTER.*

CHIQUITA CHOCOLATE PIE

1 cup sour cream

1 cup milk

1 (4 serving) box instant chocolate
    pudding

3 bananas

1 (9 inch) graham cracker piecrust

Frozen whipped topping, slightly softened

Super-Fast

In a medium bowl, mix sour cream and milk until smooth.
Add dry pudding mix, stirring until mixture is slightly
thickened and smooth. Slice two of the bananas into the
bottom of the graham cracker piecrust. Pour mixture over
bananas. Top with frozen whipped topping and remaining
sliced banana.

KENTUCKY PECAN PIE

1 cup white corn syrup

½ cup packed brown sugar

⅛ teaspoon salt

⅓ cup butter, melted

1 teaspoon vanilla extract

3 eggs, slightly beaten

1 (9 inch) piecrust, unbaked

1 cup chopped pecans

Preheat oven to 350°. In a medium bowl, combine syrup,
sugar, salt, butter, vanilla extract, and eggs. Mix well. Pour
into piecrust. Sprinkle mixture with pecans. Bake at 350°
for 40 to 45 minutes.

SNAPPY CHEESECAKE

1 box unflavored gelatin

½ cup sugar

1 cup boiling water

2 (8-ounce) packages cream cheese, softened

1 teaspoon vanilla

1 (9 inch) graham cracker piecrust

In a large bowl, combine gelatine and sugar, add boiling water and stir until gelatine is dissolved. With electric mixer, beat in cream cheese and vanilla until smooth. Pour into crust, chill until firm. Top with fresh or canned fruit.

• •

CHEESECAKE TO THE RESCUE

1 (8 ounce) package cream cheese, softened

1 (12 ounce) can sweetened condensed milk

⅓ cup lemon juice

1 (16 ounce) can cherry pie filling

1 (9 inch) graham cracker crust

In large bowl, combine cream cheese, milk, and lemon juice. Mix well.Pour mixture into crust. Top with cherry pie filling. Chill.

TO DIVIDE A PIE INTO FIVE EQUAL SLICES, FIRST CUT A "Y" INTO THE PIE. THEN CUT THE TWO LARGE PIECES IN HALF.

TASTY PEACH PIE

1 (8 ounce) package cream cheese, softened

1½ cups confectioners' sugar

1¼ teaspoons almond extract

2 cups chopped peaches

1 (8 ounce) carton frozen whipped topping, slightly softened

1 (9 inch) piecrust, baked

In a large bowl, combine cream cheese, sugar, and almond extract. Mix well. Fold in peaches and frozen whipped topping. Pour mixture into baked piecrust. Chill.

• •

LAST MINUTE PINEAPPLE PIE

1 (14 ounce) can sweetened condensed milk

1 (8 ounce) carton frozen whipped topping

½ cup chopped pecans

1 (14 ounce) can chopped pineapple, drained

1 teaspoon lemon juice

1 (9 inch) graham cracker crust

In a large bowl, combine all ingredients, except piecrust. Mix well. Pour into piecrust. Chill.

CRUNCHY LIME PIE

2 (8 ounce) packages cream cheese, softened

1 teaspoon grated lime peel

½ cup lime juice

1 (14 ounce) can sweetened condensed milk

1 pretzel crust (see page 215)

In a large bowl, using an electric mixer combine cream cheese, lime peel, lime juice, and milk. Mix until smooth and creamy. Pour mixture into piecrust. Cover and freeze. Remove from freezer 10 minutes before serving.

• •

BUTTERMILK PIE

1¼ cups sugar

3 eggs

1 tablespoon flour

6 tablespoons buttermilk

1 teaspoon vanilla extract

⅔ stick butter or margarine, melted

1 (9 inch) piecrust, unbaked

Preheat oven to 350°. In a medium bowl, combine sugar, eggs, flour, buttermilk, vanilla extract, and margarine. Mix well. Pour into piecrust. Bake at 350° for 45 to 50 minutes.

FOR CRISP PIECRUSTS, SUBSTITUTE ONE TABLESPOON OF VINEGAR FOR ONE OF THE TABLESPOONS OF WATER.

TWO PIE CRUST

½ teaspoon salt

2 cups flour

⅓ cup solid shortening

⅓ cup butter

⅓ cup ice water

In a large bowl, combine salt and flour. Using a fork, add small amounts of butter and shortening to flour, making dough. Moisten with ice water. Form into two balls, wrap in wax paper and chill until ready to roll out for crust.

QUICK PIE CRUST

1 cup flour

1 stick butter or margarine

2 tablespoons salt

Preheat oven to 350°. In a medium bowl, combine all ingredients. Form into a ball, roll into pie crust and press into a 9 inch pie pan. Bake at 350° for 12 minutes or until golden brown.

CHOCOLATE CRUMB CRUST

1½ cups vanilla wafer crumbs

½ cup confectioners' sugar

⅓ cup cocoa

⅓ cup butter or margarine, melted

In a medium bowl, combine crumbs, sugar, cocoa, and butter. Press firmly onto bottom of 9-inch springform pan.

GRAHAM CRACKER CRUST

1½ cups graham cracker crumbs

2 tablespoons sugar

6 tablespoons margarine, melted

⅛ teaspoon cinnamon

Preheat oven to 350°. In a medium bowl, combine all ingredients, mixing well. Press evenly into a 9 inch pie pan. Bake at 350° for 10 minutes. Cool.

• •

CHOCOLATE COOKIE CRUMB CRUST

1¼ cups finely crushed chocolate
   cookies

½ cup sugar

¼ cup margarine, melted

In a medium bowl, combine all ingredients, mixing well. Press evenly on bottom and sides of 9 inch pie plate. Fill as desired. Chill before serving.

• •

PRETZEL PIE CRUST

1¼ cups crushed pretzels

½ cup margarine, melted

¼ cup sugar

In a medium bowl, combine all ingredients. Firmly press mixture against bottom and sides of 9 inch pie plate. Chill until firm.

PECAN PIE CRUST

1 cup chopped pecans

1½ sticks butter, softened

1½ cups flour

2 tablespoons sugar

Preheat oven to 325°. In a medium bowl, combine pecans, butter, flour, and sugar. Roll out and pat into a 9 inch pie pan. Bake at 325° for 20 minutes or until golden brown.

• •

MERINGUE FOR PIE

3 egg whites

½ teaspoon vanilla extract

¼ teaspoon cream of tartar

6 tablespoons sugar

Bring egg whites to room temperature. In a medium bowl, combine egg whites, vanilla extract, and cream of tartar. Beat with an electric mixer on medium speed until soft peaks form. Gradually add sugar, one tablespoon at a time, beating on high speed until soft peaks form. Spread meringue over pie. Bake as directed in pie recipe.

TO USE HARD BROWN SUGAR, SCRAPE THE LUMP ON A CHEESE GRATER TO SHAVE OFF THE AMOUNT THAT IS NEEDED.

CHOCOLATE LAYERED ANGEL CAKE

1 box angel food cake mix

¼ cup cocoa

Chocolate Glaze

Prepare cake batter according to package directions. Divide cake batter into two bowls. Gradually sift cocoa over batter in one bowl, folding until well blended. Be careful not to deflate batter. Alternately spoon plain and chocolate batter into a 10 inch tube pan. Bake at 375° for 30 to 35 minutes. Cool completely. Top with chocolate glaze

Chocolate Glaze

⅓ cup sugar

¼ cup water

1 cup semi-sweet chocolate chips

In a small saucepan, combine sugar and water. Cook and stir over medium heat, until mixture comes to a boil. Add chocolate chips, stirring until chocolate melts. Cool to desired consistency. Pour over cake.

● ●

ORANGE ANGEL FOOD CAKE

Super-Fast

1 box angel food cake mix

1 teaspoon grated orange peel

½ teaspoon orange extract

Orange Glaze (see page 217)

Prepare cake batter according to package directions. Add orange peel and orange extract to batter. Bake as directed on package. Cool. Remove from pan and invert onto a serving plate. Pour Orange Glaze over cake.

Orange Glaze

¼ cup butter

2 cups confectioners' sugar

4 tablespoons orange juice

In a small saucepan over low heat, melt butter until it foams and turns a rich brown color. In a small bowl, combine sugar and melted butter. Stir in orange juice, mixing well. Immediately pour over cooled cake, allowing glaze to drizzle down sides.

MOM'S FRUIT COCKTAIL CAKE

2 cups all-purpose flour

1⅓ cups sugar

3 teaspoons baking soda

1 (19 ounce) can fruit cocktail

2 eggs

1 teaspoon vanilla extract

½ teaspoon salt

Cake Topping (see below)

Preheat oven to 350°. Spray a 13 x 9 inch baking pan with non-stick vegetable spray. In a large bowl, combine all ingredients, mixing well. Pour into prepared pan. Bake at 350° for 45 minutes or until cake springs back in the center when touched. Cool on wire rack. Pour topping over cooled cake.

Fruit Cocktail Cake Topping

8 tablespoons butter

1 cup packed brown sugar

½ cup milk

In a small saucepan, combine all ingredients, cooking over low heat for 5 minutes. Pour warm topping over cake.

APPLE AND SAUCE CAKE

2 cups grated apples

1 cup sugar

1 egg

1 cup flour

1¼ teaspoons baking soda

1 teaspoon cinnamon

Apple Sauce Topping (see below)

Preheat oven to 350°. Lightly grease an 8 x 8 inch baking pan. Set aside. In a large bowl, combine apples and sugar. Let stand 10 minutes. Add egg, flour, baking soda, and cinnamon. Mix well. Pour into prepared pan. Bake at 350° for 20 to 25 minutes. Cool. Serve with apple sauce.

Apple Sauce Cake Topping

½ cup butter

½ cup cream

1 cup sugar

1 teaspoon vanilla extract

In a medium saucepan, combine all ingredients. Cook and stir until mixture comes to a boil. Boil for 2 minutes. Serve over apple cake.

USE A DOILY TO MAKE A SNOWFLAKE PATTERN ON TOP OF AN UNFROSTED CAKE. PLACE THE DOILY ON TOP OF THE CAKE AND SIFT CONFECTIONER'S SUGAR ONTO THE DOILY UNTIL ALL THE SPACES IN THE DOILY ARE FILLED WITH SUGAR. CAREFULLY REMOVE THE DOILY TO REVEAL YOUR DESIGN.

MOTHER-IN-LAW'S CHOCOLATE CAKE

2 eggs

1½ cups sour cream

1½ cups flour

1⅓ cups sugar

3 tablespoons cocoa

1½ teaspoons baking soda

⅛ teaspoon salt

1 teaspoon vanilla

Preheat oven to 350°. Lightly grease and flour a 13 x 9 x 2 inch baking pan. Set aside. In a medium bowl, beat eggs and sour cream. Set aside. In a large bowl, sift flour, sugar, cocoa, baking soda, and salt. Add egg mixture to dry mixture, mixing well. Add vanilla extract. Pour into prepared baking pan. Bake at 350° for 35 minutes, or until cake is done.

ANGEL PEACH BERRY CAKE

1 cup heavy cream

1 cup frozen raspberries, partially thawed

1 angel food cake

1½ cups sliced peaches

In a chilled bowl, using chilled beaters, whip cream until stiff peaks form. Fold in berries. Spread over cake. Arrange Authors note:peach slices around edges and on top of cake.

AUTHOR'S NOTE: THESE ARE TWO FAVORITE RECIPES FROM OUR BEST SELLING *BUSY WOMAN COOKBOOK.*

ICE CREAM CONE CAKES

1 box chocolate or yellow cake mix

24 flat-bottom ice cream cones
    frosting

½ cup sprinkles

Prepare cake mix as directed on package. Spoon about ¼ cup batter into each cone. Set cones on baking sheet. Bake at 350 degrees for 25 minutes. Cool on rack. Spoon frosting over cakes. Garnish with sprinkles, if desired. Kids will love these cupcakes.

MIRACLE WHIP® CHOCOLATE CAKE

1 cup Miracle Whip®

3 eggs

1 box devils' food cake mix

1⅓ cups water

Combine all ingredients and mix well. Pour into greased 13 x 9 inch cake pan. Bake at 350 degrees for 35 to 40 minutes.

VANILLA PUDDING CAKE

1 box yellow cake mix

2 (4 serving) boxes instant vanilla pudding

5 eggs

½ cup water

½ cup milk

½ cup vegetable oil

Preheat oven to 350°. Spray a 13 x 9 x 2 inch baking pan with non-stick cooking spray. Set aside. In a large bowl, using an electric mixer, combine all ingredients, beating for two minutes. Pour batter into prepared pan. Bake at 350° for 55 minutes, or until cake tests done. Cool on wire rack.

• •

YUMMY PUMPKIN CAKE

Note: This recipe makes 2 cakes
1 (16 ounce) can pumpkin

1 box yellow cake mix

4 eggs

½ cup vegetable oil

1 (11 ounce) can mandarin oranges with juice

Preheat oven to 325°. Lightly grease and flour four 8-inch round cake pans. Set aside. In a large bowl, combine pumpkin, cake mix, eggs, oil, and mandarin oranges and juice. Mix well. Pour batter into prepared cake pans. Place 2 pans at a time in the oven and bake at 325° for 30 minutes. Frost as desired.

ONLY THE BEST CARROT CAKE

2 cups sugar

2 cups flour

2 teaspoons baking soda

2 teaspoons cinnamon

1 teaspoon salt

1½ cups oil

4 eggs, beaten

3 cups shredded carrots

Cream Cheese Icing (see below)

Preheat oven to 350°. Spray a 13 x 9 x 2 inch baking pan with non-stick cooking spray. Set aside. Sift dry ingredients into a large bowl. Add oil and eggs, mixing well. Stir in carrots. Pour into prepared pan. Bake for 30 to 35 minutes or until cake tests done. Serve with Cream Cheese Icing.

Cream Cheese Icing

1 (8 ounce) package cream cheese, softened

½ stick margarine, softened

1 (1 pound) box confectioners' sugar, sifted

1 teaspoon vanilla extract

Chopped nuts (optional)

Using an electric mixer, beat cream cheese until smooth. In a separate bowl, combine margarine and sugar, mixing well. Stir mixture into cream cheese. Add vanilla extract and beat until smooth. Frost cool cake. Top with nuts, if desired.

THANKSGIVING PUMPKIN CAKE

1 box yellow cake mix

1 (4 serving) box instant butterscotch pudding

4 eggs

¼ cup water

¼ cup vegetable oil

1 cup canned pumpkin

1 teaspoon cinnamon

¼ teaspoon ginger

Creamy Topping (see below)

Preheat oven to 350°. Lightly grease and flour a 10 inch tube pan. Set aside. Combine all ingredients in a large bowl. Using an electric mixer, blend on low speed, then mix at medium speed for 5 minutes. Pour into prepared tube pan. Bake at 350° for 50 to 55 minutes, or until cake tests done. Cool on wire rack. Cover with creamy topping.

Creamy Topping

1½ cups half and half

½ cup milk

1 (4 serving) box instant vanilla pudding

In a medium bowl, combine half and half and milk. Add instant pudding. Using an electric mixer, beat on low speed for 2 minutes. Chill. Spread on cooled cake.

TEST BAKING POWDER OR BAKING SODA BY PLACING A TEASPOON IN HOT WATER. IF IT FIZZLES, IT IS STILL GOOD.

ANGEL FOOD CAKE FROSTING

1 cup sugar

¾ cup cream

¼ cup butter, softened

In a small saucepan, combine sugar and cream, bringing to a boil. Lower heat. Cook and stir for 2 minutes. Remove from heat and add butter, mixing well. Spread warm frosting over angel food cake.

For a pretty dessert, use a prepared angel food cake, spread warm frosting over the cake and top slices with strawberries, raspberries, or peaches.

● ●

EASY CHOCOLATE FROSTING

6 tablespoons margarine

6 tablespoons milk

1½ cups sugar

1 cup milk chocolate chips

In a medium saucepan, combine margarine, milk, and sugar. Cook and stir, bringing mixture to a boil. Cook for 2 minutes. Place chocolate chips in a medium bowl. Pour hot mixture over chips and beat until mixture is smooth and ready to spread over cake.

SMOOTH CHOCOLATE FROSTING

Super-Fast

2 cups whipping cream

2 cups milk chocolate chips

3½ cups confectioners' sugar

In a large saucepan, warm cream over low heat. Remove from heat and stir in chocolate until melted. Place pan in a bowl of ice water, stirring until mixture cools. Whisk in sugar, small amounts at a time, until mixture is smooth and thick.

WHIPPED WHITE FROSTING

1 egg white

¾ cup sugar

¼ teaspoon cream of tartar

1 teaspoon vanilla extract

¼ cup boiling water

In a medium bowl, combine egg white, sugar, cream of tartar, and vanilla extract. Mix well. Add water. Using an electric mixer, mix on medium speed for 4 minutes or until frosting is thick.

COCONUT FROSTING

1 cup packed brown sugar

¼ cup milk

1 stick butter

1 cup shredded coconut

In a medium saucepan, combine sugar, milk, and butter. Cook and stir over low heat for 5 minutes. Add coconut. Cook until mixture is warm. Pour over cake while frosting is still warm.

CLASSIC WHITE FROSTING

¼ cup margarine

¼ cup solid shortening

1 egg white

2 teaspoons vanilla extract

2 cups confectioners' sugar

In a medium bowl, combine all ingredients using an electric mixer on medium speed. Turn mixer to high speed and beat until frosting is creamy.

• •

CHOCOLATE CHIP COOKIES

2 sticks margarine

¾ cup sugar

¾ cup packed brown sugar

2 eggs

½ teaspoon water

1 teaspoon vanilla extract

2¼ cups flour

1 teaspoon baking soda

1 teaspoon salt

1 (12 ounce) package semi-sweet chocolate chips

Preheat oven to 350°. Coat cookie sheets with non-stick cooking spray. Set aside. In a large bowl, cream margarine, sugar, brown sugar, water, and vanilla extract. Add eggs, one at a time, beating after each addition. Add flour, soda, and salt, blending well. Stir in chocolate chips. Drop by teaspoonfuls onto prepared cookie sheet. Bake at 350° for 10 to 12 minutes. Do not overbake. Let stand 2 minutes. Remove to wire racks to cool.

CHOCOLATE SURPRISE COOKIES

2 egg whites

⅓ cup sugar

⅛ teaspoon cream of tartar

⅛ teaspoon salt

½ teaspoon vanilla extract

½ cup nuts

1 cup semi-sweet chocolate chips

Preheat oven to 250°. Lightly grease a cookie sheet. Set aside. In a medium bowl, using an electric mixer, beat egg whites, sugar, and cream of tartar until stiff peaks form. Fold in salt, vanilla extract, nuts, and chocolate chips. Drop by teaspoon onto a greased cookie sheet. Bake for 30 minutes.

CHOCOLATE DROP COOKIES

Super-Fast

1 (12 ounce) package milk chocolate chips

3 tablespoons butter

1 (14 ounce) can sweetened condensed milk

1 cup flour

1 cup chopped nuts

Preheat oven to 350°. Lightly grease a cookie sheet. Set aside. In the top of a double boiler, melt chocolate chips and butter. Add milk, flour, and nuts. Mix well. Drop by teaspoonful onto prepared cookie sheet. Bake at 350° for 8 to 10 minutes.

CHEWY COCONUT MACAROONS

5⅓ cups shredded coconut

½ cup cocoa

1 (14 ounce) can sweetened
 condensed milk

2 teaspoons vanilla extract

24 candied red cherries, cut in half

Preheat oven to 350°. Lightly coat a cookie sheet with non-stick cooking spray. Set aside. In a large bowl, combine coconut and cocoa. Stir in milk and vanilla extract until well blended. Drop by rounded teaspoon onto prepared cookie sheet. Press a cherry half into the center of each cookie. Bake at 350° for 8 to 10 minutes. Immediately place on wire racks to cool.

CHEESECAKE COOKIES

1 cup butter, softened

2 (3 ounce) packages cream
 cheese, softened

2 cups sugar

2 cups flour

1 cup chopped pecans

Preheat oven to 350°. In a large bowl, using an electric mixer, cream butter and cream cheese. Add sugar, beating until mixture is fluffy. Add flour, mixing well. Fold in pecans. Drop by teaspoonful onto ungreased cookie sheet. Bake at 350° for 12 minutes. Cool on wire racks.

EASY TO ROLL SUGAR COOKIES

2 sticks margarine, softened

1½ cups confectioners' sugar

1 egg

1 teaspoon vanilla extract

2½ cups flour

1 teaspoon soda

1 teaspoon cream of tartar

¼ teaspoon salt

Frosting (See below)

Preheat oven to 375°. In a large bowl, cream margarine, sugar, egg, and vanilla extract. Add flour, soda, cream of tartar, and salt. Mix well. Roll out on floured board. Cut into desired shapes. Bake at 375° for 8 to 10 minutes. Do not overbake. Cool on wire racks. Frost when cookies are cool.

Sugar Cookie Frosting

¼ cup margarine

1½ teaspoons vanilla extract

3 cups confectioners' sugar

¼ cup milk

In a small bowl, using an electric mixer, combine all ingredients. Mix on low speed until smooth. Tint with food coloring, if desired. Frost cooled cookies.

KEEP COOKIES CRISP IN THE COOKIE JAR BY PLACING A HANDFUL OF SHREDDED TISSUE PAPER IN THE BOTTOM.

BUTTER COOKIES FOR A PARTY

8 sticks butter (do not use margarine)

4 cups confectioners' sugar

9 cups flour

4 teaspoons vanilla extract

2 cups chopped pecans

Preheat oven to 350°. In a large bowl, cream butter and sugar. Alternately add flour, vanilla extract, and pecans. Mix well. Roll dough into walnut-sized balls and place on ungreased cookie sheet. Press with a fork. Bake at 350° for 20 minutes.

• •

CAN'T BE A COOKIE

Super-Fast

1 cup sugar

1 cup peanut butter

1 teaspoon vanilla extract

1 egg

Preheat oven to 350°. In a medium bowl, combine sugar, peanut butter, vanilla extract, and egg. Drop by heaping teaspoon onto greased cookie sheet. Using a fork, criss cross each cookie. Bake at 350° for 10 minutes. Cool on wire racks.

USE CLEAN, EMPTY KETCHUP OR MUSTARD SQUEEZE BOTTLES AS A CAKE-DECORATING TOOL. SIMPLY FILL WITH FROSTING AND USE THE BOTTLE TO MAKE DESIGNS OR WRITE ON TOP OF YOUR CAKE.

QUICK OATMEAL COOKIES

1 cup flour

1 cup butter

½ cup sugar

1½ cups quick oatmeal

Confectioners' sugar

Preheat oven to 350°. In a large bowl, combine all ingredients except confectioners' sugar, mixing well. Roll into walnut sized balls. Place on ungreased cookie sheet. Flatten. Bake at 350° for 10 to 12 minutes. Cool on wire racks. Dust with confectioners' sugar.

• •

CUPCAKE BROWNIES

2 sticks margarine

2 squares bakers chocolate

1 cup chopped nuts

4 eggs

1¾ cups sugar

1 cup flour

1 teaspoon vanilla extract

Preheat oven to 350°. Lightly grease and flour muffin tins. Set aside. In a saucepan over low heat, melt margarine and chocolate, stirring to avoid scorching. Stir in nuts. Remove from heat. In a large bowl, combine eggs, sugar, flour, and vanilla extract. Gently blend with a spoon. Add chocolate mixture and blend again, just until all ingredients are combined. Do not overmix. Fill muffin cups ⅔ full. Bake at 350 ° for 30 minutes.

QUICK SNACK CHEERIOS® BARS

⅓ cup light corn syrup

1 (6 ounce) package semi-sweet
    chocolate chips

1 teaspoon vanilla extract

4 cups Cheerios®

Grease a 9 x 9 x 2 inch baking dish and set aside. In a large
saucepan, heat syrup to boiling. Remove from heat. Add
chocolate chips and vanilla extract, stirring until chocolate
melts. Add Cheerios® a small amount at a time, stirring
until cereal is coated. Pour mixture into prepared baking
dish. Cool for 1 hour. Cut into bars.

• •

PEANUT BUTTER SQUARES

1 cup peanut butter

1 stick margarine, softened

3 eggs, beaten

2 cups packed brown sugar

1 cup flour

½ teaspoon salt

1 teaspoon vanilla extract

Preheat oven to 350°. Lightly grease a 9 x 9 x 2 inch baking
pan. Set aside. In a medium bowl, cream peanut butter and
margarine. Add eggs, brown sugar, flour, salt, and vanilla
extract. Mix well. Press mixture into prepared pan. Bake at
350° for 20 to 25 minutes. Cool and cut into bars.

IMMEDIATELY COVER YOUR BROWNIES WHEN THEY COME OUT OF THE OVEN. THIS KEEPS THEM MOIST.

NUTTY CHOCO BARS

½ cup butter, softened

½ cup packed brown sugar

1½ cups flour

¼ teaspoon salt

¾ cup peanut butter

Frosting (see below)

Preheat oven to 350°. Lightly grease a 13 x 9 x 2 inch baking pan. Set aside. In a large bowl, using an electric mixer on medium speed, cream butter and sugar. In a separate bowl, combine flour and salt. Add to creamed mixture. Press mixture into prepared pan. Spread with peanut butter. Cool in pan. Top with Chocolate Frosting.

Chocolate Frosting

1 cup chocolate chips

2 tablespoons light corn syrup

2 tablespoons water

1 cup chopped pecans

In top of a double boiler melt chips. Add syrup and water, mixing well. Stir in nuts. Spread over cooled peanut butter bars.

PRIZE WINNING BROWNIES

2 sticks butter, melted

2 cups sugar

2 teaspoons vanilla extract

4 eggs

¾ cup cocoa

1 cup all-purpose flour

½ teaspoon baking powder

¼ teaspoon salt

Preheat oven to 350°. Lightly grease a 13 x 9 x 2 inch baking pan. Set aside. In a large bowl, combine melted butter, sugar, and vanilla extract. Add eggs, one at a time, beating well after each addition. Add cocoa. Mix until well blended. Add flour, baking powder, and salt, beating well. Pour into greased baking pan. Bake for 30 to 35 minutes. Cool and cut into bars.

HELLO DOLLIES SQUARES

1 stick butter or margarine

1½ cups graham cracker crumbs

1½ cups flaked coconut

1½ cups chocolate chips

1 cup nuts

1 (14 ounce) can sweetened condensed milk

Preheat oven to 350°. Melt butter in a 13 x 9 x 2 inch baking pan. Layer graham cracker crumbs, coconut, chocolate chips, and nuts over melted butter. Pour milk over mixture. Bake at 350° for 30 minutes. Cool and cut into squares.

OATMEAL CARAMEL SQUARES

1 box white cake mix

2 cups uncooked oats

½ cup packed brown sugar

1 cup vegetable oil

1 egg

¾ cup caramel ice cream topping

Preheat oven to 350°. Lightly grease a 13 x 9 x 2 inch baking pan. Set aside. In a large bowl, combine cake mix, oats, and brown sugar. Add oil and egg, mixing well. Press half the mixture into the bottom of prepared baking pan. Spread caramel topping over mixture. Crumble rest of mixture over caramel topping, covering entire top. Bake at 350° for 30 to 35 minutes or until golden brown. Cool and cut into bars.

● ●

BETTER THAN A MIX BROWNIES

1 stick margarine

1 cup sugar

4 eggs

1 (16 ounce) can chocolate syrup

1 cup plus 1 tablespoon flour

Brownie Frosting (see below)

Preheat oven to 350°. Lightly grease a 15 x 10 x 1 inch jelly roll pan. Set aside. In a large bowl, combine all ingredients. Pour into prepared pan. Bake at 350° for 20 minutes. Cool and frost.

BROWNIE FROSTING

3 tablespoons margarine

¾ cup sugar

3 tablespoons milk

¼ cup chocolate chips

In a medium saucepan, combine margarine, sugar, and milk. Boil for 3 minutes. Remove from heat. Add chocolate chips, stirring until melted. Beat to spreading consistency and frost cooled brownies.

• •

CHOCOLATE CARAMEL BARS

1 box German chocolate cake mix

¾ cup margarine, melted

⅔ cup sweetened condensed milk

1 cup chopped nuts

1 (14 ounce) package caramels

1 cup chocolate chips

Preheat oven to 350°. Lightly grease a 13 x 9 x 2 inch baking pan. Set aside. In a medium bowl, combine cake mix, margarine, and ⅓ cup of the milk. Mix well. Spread half the mixture into prepared baking pan. Bake at 350° for 8 minutes. Remove from oven. In a small saucepan, melt chocolate. In another saucepan, melt caramels in the remaining milk. Spread chocolate over cake. Top with caramel mixture. Drizzle remaining cake batter over top mixture. Bake an additional 15 to 20 minutes. Cool and cut into bars.

CHOCOLATE CEREAL SQUARES

½ cup light corn syrup

4 (1.5 ounce) milk chocolate bars,
    broken into small pieces

½ teaspoon vanilla extract

3½ cups honey graham cereal

1 cup miniature marshmallows

Lightly butter an 8-inch square baking pan. Set aside. Microwave syrup to boiling point. Remove bowl from microwave, add chocolate and vanilla extract, stirring until chocolate melts. In a large bowl, pour chocolate mixture over cereal, coating all pieces well. Add marshmallows. Mix well. Press mixture into prepared pan. Chill until firm. Cut into squares.

• •

CHOCOLATE SNACK CAKE

1 box Devil's food cake mix

1 cup white chocolate chips, divided

½ cup semisweet chocolate chips

Preheat oven to 350°. Prepare cake mix as directed on package. Stir in ½ cup white chocolate chips and semisweet chips. Pour into greased and floured 13 x 9 x 2 inch pan. Bake for 35 to 40 minutes. Remove from oven. Sprinkle top with remaining white chocolate chips. Serve watm. Makes 12 to 16 servings.

BROWN QUICK-COOKING OATS IN A LITTLE BUTTER, THEN USE THEM AS A SUBSTITUTE FOR CHOPPED NUTS IN COOKIE RECIPES.

SHORT CUT PEACH COBBLER

1 box yellow cake mix

1 (29 ounce) can peaches, with juice

1 stick butter or margarine, melted

Preheat oven to 350 degrees. In 9 x 13 inch baking pan, pour peaches. Sprinkle ¾ cake mix over peaches. Pour butter evenly over top. Bake 40 to 50 minutes.

• •

BAKED APPLE CRISP

4 tart apples

1 cup flour

1 cup sugar

1 teaspoon baking powder

1 teaspoon cinnamon

⅛ teaspoon salt

1 egg

½ cup melted butter

Preheat oven to 375°. Wash, pare, and slice apples. Place in an 8 x 8 inch baking dish. Set aside. In a large bowl, combine flour, sugar, baking powder, cinnamon, and salt. Cut egg into mixture. Crumble mixture over apples. Drizzle with melted butter. Bake at 375° for 40 to 45 minutes.

BAKED CHERRY CRISP

2 tablespoons butter

1 cup flour

1 cup sugar

½ cup juice from canned cherries

2 cups cherries, unsweetened

Super-Fast

Preheat oven to 375°. Lightly butter a 9 x 9 x 2 inch baking pan. Set aside. In a medium bowl, combine flour, sugar, and cherry juice. Add cherries. Pour mixture into baking pan. Spread crumb mixture over top. Bake at 375° for 20 to 25 minutes. Serve with frozen whipped topping.

Crumb Topping for Cherry Crisp

1 cup sugar

¾ cup flour

7 tablespoons butter

¼ teaspoon nutmeg

In a small bowl, combine sugar, flour, butter, and nutmeg. Mix well. Crumble over cherry mixture before baking.

TO KEEP BROWN SUGAR FROM LUMPING, REMOVE IT FROM THE ORIGINAL CONTAINER AND STORE IN A TIGHTLY SEALED GLASS JAR.

FUDGE CHEESECAKE

2 cups semi-sweet chocolate chips

3 (8 ounce) packages cream cheese, softened

1 (14 ounce) can sweetened condensed milk

4 eggs

2 teaspoons vanilla extract

1 (9 inch) chocolate crumb crust

Preheat oven to 300°. Microwave chocolate chips on high until melted. In a large bowl, beat cream cheese until fluffy. Gradually beat in milk until smooth. Add melted chocolate, mixing well. Add eggs, one at a time, beating after each addition. Add vanilla extract. Pour into chocolate crumb crust. Bake at 300 ° for one hour, or until center is set.

• •

PEACHY PUDDING

1 (4 serving) box peach gelatin

½ cup hot milk

1½ cups cold milk

1 (4 serving) box instant vanilla pudding

Peach slices

Whipped topping

In a small bowl, dissolve gelatin in hot milk. Set aside. In a medium bowl, using an electric mixer combine cold milk and pudding, mixing on low speed for 2 minutes. Fold in gelatin mixture, mixing well. Let stand 5 minutes. Spoon into individual serving dishes. Garnish with peach slices and whipped topping.

FRIED PEACHES AND ICE CREAM

2 large peaches, firm and not too ripe

2 tablespoons butter, melted

2 tablespoons sugar

Ice cream

Peel and halve peaches. Place peaches (cut side down) in skillet with melted butter. Cook until edges are brown, turning and sprinkling cut side with half the sugar. Cook until brown. Sprinkle with remaining sugar. Cook over low heat until sugar carmelizes, slightly. Turn once to coat. Serve with ice cream.

• •

PINEAPPLE ORANGE DESSERT

Super-Fast

1 (15 ounce) can crushed pineapple, undrained

1 (4 serving box) orange flavored gelatin

2 cups buttermilk

1 (8 ounce) carton frozen whipped topping

In a large saucepan, heat pineapple and add gelatin, stirring until gelatin dissolves. Remove from heat. Cool 20 minutes. Add buttermilk and whipped topping. Mix well. Chill until firm.

STRAWBERRY DAZZLE

2 pints fresh strawberries

⅓ cup sugar

⅓ cup orange flavored liqueur

1 (8 ounce) carton frozen whipped topping

Super-Fast

Wash and hull strawberries. Pat dry and set aside. In a large bowl, combine sugar and orange liqueur, stirring until sugar dissolves. Fold in strawberries, stirring just to coat. Cover and chill. Serve in individual dishes, with frozen whipped topping. Makes 6 servings.

● ●

CHERRY WHIPPED DESSERT

1 (20 ounce) can cherry pie filling

1 (6 ounce) can crushed pineapple, drained

1 (12 ounce) can sweetened condensed milk

1 (8 ounce) carton frozen whipped topping

Combine all ingredients. Chill until firm. Makes 6 servings.

FOR PERFECT WHIPPED CREAM, CHILL CREAM, BEATER AND BOWL BEFORE WHIPPING.

UNEXPECTED COMPANY DESSERT

3 cups canned thick cherries

1 (9 inch) graham cracker crust

2 cups frozen whipped topping, slightly thawed

3 graham crackers, crushed

Pour cherries into graham cracker crust. Spread whipped topping over cherries. Sprinkle with crushed graham crackers. Chill slightly.

CRUNCHY CHOCOLATE SUNDAE

¼ cup margarine or butter

1 cup chopped walnuts

1 (6 ounce) package semi-sweet chocolate chips

½ teaspoon vanilla extract

1 quart vanilla ice cream

Melt butter in a medium skillet. Add walnuts. Cook and stir over medium heat until butter is light brown. Remove from heat. Add chocolate chips and vanilla extract, stirring until chocolate melts. Serve warm over vanilla ice cream.

CRUSHED PINEAPPLE CREAM

*1 (13½ ounce) can crushed
    pineapple, undrained*

30 marshmallows, chopped

1 cup whipped cream

In a large saucepan, heat pineapple and juice. Add marshmallows. Cook and stir over low heat until marshmallows melt. Remove from heat. Cool until partially set. Fold in whipped cream. Makes 4 to 6 servings.

FRUIT FREEZE DESSERT

*1 (8 ounce) package cream
    cheese, softened*

*1 (20 ounce) can crushed
    pineapple, drained*

*1 (10 ounce) package frozen strawberries,
    thawed with juice*

2 bananas, sliced and quartered

1 (8 ounce) carton frozen whipped topping

In a large bowl, combine all ingredients. Pour into a
13 x 9 inch baking pan and freeze until firm.

• •

HOME MADE ICE CREAM

6 eggs

1 cup sugar

4 tablespoons white corn syrup

1 (14 ounce) can sweetened condensed milk

*Milk to fill a one gallon ice cream freezer
    container 4 inches from the top*

In a large bowl, using an electric mixer, beat eggs and sugar
until well blended. Add syrup, condensed milk, and whole
milk. Pour into freezer container and mix according to
freezer instructions. Let set 1 hour before serving.

FRUIT ICE CREAM

8 eggs

2 (14 ounce) cans sweetened condensed milk

1 pint half and half

1 quart fruit puree (strawberries or peaches)

Sugar

In a large bowl, using an electric mixer, beat eggs on high. Add milk and beat for 10 minutes. Add fruit and sweeten as desired. Pour into ice cream freezer and prepare according to freezer directions. Makes 1 gallon.

BANANA AND WAFERS PUDDING

Super-Fast

2 (4 serving) boxes instant vanilla pudding

1 (16 ounce) carton frozen whipped topping

1 (14 ounce) can sweetened condensed milk

4 bananas, sliced

Wafer cookies

Prepare pudding according to package directions. Fold in half the whipped topping. Add condensed milk and bananas. In a large bowl, layer wafers, then mixture. Top with remaining frozen whipped topping. Makes 8 servings.

SPRINKLE CONFECTIONERS' SUGAR ONTO THE SERVING PLATE TO KEEP YOUR CAKE FROM SLIDING WHEN IT IS SERVED.

OUT OF THE PAST CUSTARD

4 eggs

½ cup sugar

1 quart milk

1 teaspoon vanilla extract

Preheat oven to 250°. In a large bowl, combine eggs and sugar, beating well. Add milk and vanilla extract. Mix well. Fill custard cups ⅔ full. Place in shallow pan of hot water. Set in oven and bake at 250° for 1½ hours or until firm.

• •

MACAROON INDULGENCE

1½ cups cold milk

1 cup sour cream

¼ teaspoon almond extract

1 (4 serving) box instant vanilla pudding

½ cup crumbled macaroon cookies

In a medium bowl, combine milk, sour cream, and almond extract. Using a wire whisk, mix well. Add pudding and mix until blended. Spoon half the mixture into individual dessert dishes. Sprinkle crumbled macaroons over pudding. Top with remaining pudding. Chill. Garnish with additional crumbs before serving. Makes 4 servings.

STORING A CANDY THERMOMETER UPRIGHT WILL KEEP THE MERCURY FROM SEPARATING.

VANILLA MILK CHIPS FUDGE

Super-Fast

1½ cups vanilla chocolate chips

⅔ cup sweetened condensed milk

1½ cups chopped almonds, toasted

½ teaspoon vanilla extract

Butter an 8 inch square pan. Set aside. In a medium sauce-pan, combine chips and milk, cook and stir over low heat until mixture is smooth. Remove from heat. Stir in almonds and vanilla extract. Spread mixture in prepared pan. Cover. Refrigerate until firm. Cut into 1-inch squares.

CHOCOLATE CHIP NUT CLUSTERS

Super-Fast

1 cup milk chocolate chips

1 teaspoon solid shortening

1 cup chopped walnuts

In a medium bowl, combine chocolate chips and shortening. Microwave on high for 1 to 1½ minutes or until mixture is smooth when stirred. Add nuts. Drop by teaspoon into 1-inch paper candy cups. Fill each cup half full. Chill until firm.

CRUNCHY FUDGE DROPS

Super-Fast

1 (12 ounce) package semi-sweet chocolate chips

¼ cup margarine

3½ cups granola (without raisins)

½ cup chopped dried fruit

In a medium saucepan, melt chocolate and margarine over low heat. Stir frequently until mixture is smooth. Remove from heat. Add cereal and dried fruit. Stir until cereal is coated. Drop by heaping teaspoons onto a waxed paper lined cookie sheet. Chill until set.

● ●

QUICK PEANUT BUTTER FUDGE

3 cups packed brown sugar

1 cup evaporated milk

1 cup peanut butter

In a medium saucepan, combine sugar and milk. Bring to a boil, stirring constantly. Lower heat and cook for 20 minutes or until mixture forms a soft ball. Remove from heat and add peanut butter. Do not stir. Let cool. When cool, beat by hand until fudge loses its gloss. Pour into buttered 8-inch square pan. Cut into squares.

SPRAY CUPCAKE LINERS WITH NON-STICK COOKING SPRAY AND THE CUPCAKES CAN BE REMOVED WITHOUT STICKING TO THE PAPER.

ELECTRIC SKILLET PEANUT BUTTER FUDGE

2 cups sugar

3 tablespoons margarine

½ cup evaporated milk

1 cup miniature marshmallows

1 cup peanut butter

1 teaspoon vanilla extract

In an electric skillet set at 280°, combine sugar, margarine, and milk. Boil 5 minutes, stirring constantly. Turn off heat and add marshmallows, peanut butter, and vanilla extract. Stir until marshmallows melt and mixture is well blended. Pour into buttered 8 inch square pan. Cool. Cut into squares.

• •

ANYTIME PEANUT BRITTLE

2 cups sugar

1 cup white corn syrup

½ cup water

1 tablespoon butter

2 cups raw peanuts

1½ teaspoons baking soda

1 teaspoon vanilla extract

In a large saucepan, combine sugar, syrup, and water. Cook to soft ball stage. Add butter and peanuts, cooking until syrup turns golden brown (hard crack). Add soda and vanilla extract. Mix well and pour into buttered 8 inch square pan, spreading thinly. Cool and break into pieces.

MICROWAVE PRALINES

1½ cups packed brown sugar

⅔ cup cream

⅛ teaspoon salt

2 tablespoons butter

1½ cups pecans

In a 3 quart microwave safe casserole, combine sugar, cream, salt, and butter. Mix well. Microwave on high for 5 minutes. Stir. Cook 4 to 5 more minutes to soft ball stage. Add pecans. Cool 1 minute. Beat until creamy. Drop by teaspoon onto waxed paper. Let set until firm. Makes 24 pralines.

• •

OLD TIME DIVINITY

4 cups sugar

1 cup light corn syrup

¾ cup water

3 egg whites

1 teaspoon vanilla extract

½ cup finely chopped nuts

In a medium saucepan, boil syrup to 255 °. Slowly add beaten egg whites. Continue beating until mixture loses gloss. Add vanilla extract and nuts. Drop by teaspoon onto waxed paper.

TO KEEP COOKIES OR GINGERBREAD SOFT, PLACE AN APPLE SLICE IN THE STORAGE CONTAINER.

HOT FUDGE SAUCE

⅓ cup cocoa

1 cup sugar

1 cup light corn syrup

½ cup light cream

¼ teaspoon salt

3 tablespoons margarine

1 teaspoon vanilla extract

In a large saucepan, combine cocoa, sugar, syrup, cream, salt, and margarine. Cook and stir over low heat until mixture comes to a full boil. Cook 3 minutcs, stirring twice. Remove from heat. Add vanilla extract. Serve this thick sauce over ice cream or brownies.

VANILLA ICE CREAM TOPPING

Super-Fast

1 (7 ounce) jar marshmallow cream

¼ cup milk

½ cup chocolate chips

In a small saucepan, combine marshmallow cream and milk. Cook and stir over low heat until mixture is well blended. Remove from heat. Add chocolate chips, stirring until melted. Serve warm or cold over vanilla ice cream. Makes 2 cups.

TINTED COCONUT

3 or 4 drops food color

2 tablespoons water

1 cup shredded coconut

In a pint jar, mix food coloring and water. Add coconut. Shake well until coconut is well coated. Use as topping for cakes, cupcakes, and fruit salads.

IF COOKIES GET TOO HARD PUT THEM IN A PLASTIC BAG WITH A PIECE OF BREAD AND LEAVE OVERNIGHT. THE NEXT MORNING, THE COOKIES SHOULD BE SOFT.

DESSERT FOR AN ANGEL

1 round (10 inches in diameter) angel food cake

1 (14 ounce) can sweetened condensed milk

⅓ cup lime juice

1 teaspoon grated lime peel

1 (12 ounce) carton frozen whipped topping

1 cup flaked coconut

Cut angel food cake horizontally into 3 layers. In medium bowl, combine milk, lime juice, and lime peel. Beat until smooth and thickened. Fold in whipped topping. Spread mixture evenly over top of first layer of cake. Place second layer of cake on bottom layer, spread evenly with mixture. Frost top and sides of cake. Sprinkle with coconut. Makes 16 servings.

Per serving: Calories-245, Protein-5gm, Fat-5 gm, Carbs-45gm, Cholesterol-10 mg, Sodium-330 mg

TIP: FROST CAKES ONLY AFTER IT HAS THROUGHLY COOLED.

PEANUT BUTTER PIE

1 (3 ounce) package fat-free cream cheese, softened

⅓ cup reduced-fat peanut butter

½ cup confectioner's sugar

¼ cup fat-free milk

1 (8 ounce) carton fat-free frozen whipped topping, thawed

1 (9 inch) chocolate crumb crust

In a large bowl, beat cream cheese until fluffy. Fold in peanut butter and sugar. Gradually add milk. Mix well. Fold in whipped topping. Spoon into piecrust. Refrigerate until ready to serve. Makes 8 servings.

Per Serving: Calories-280, Protein-6 gm, Fat-12 gm, Carbohydrates-35 gm, Cholesterol-2 mg, Sodium-325 mg.

YES YOU CAN COOKIE

1 (18 ounce) package chocolate chip cookie dough

¼ cup chopped maraschino cherries, well drained

1 tablespoon all purpose flour

2 cups Wheaties® cereal, broken into pieces

Preheat oven to 350 degrees. In large bowl, crumble cookie dough. Add cherries and flour. Mix well. Drop heaping teaspoonfuls of dough into cereal crumbs. Coat well, press cereal into dough. Shape into balls; place 2 inches apart on ungreased cookie sheets bake 12 to 15 minutes or until golden brown. Makes 20 cookies.

Per serving (1 cookie): Calories-130, Protein-1gm, Fat-6gm, Carbohydrates-18gm, Cholesterol-5gm, Sodium-115mg

FUDGE BROWNIE COOKIES

⅓ *cup confectioner's sugar*

⅛ *teaspoon cinnamon*

1 (18 ounce) package fudge brownie mix

⅓ *cup water*

Super-Fast

Preheat oven to 375°. In a small bowl, combine confectioner's sugar and cinnamon. Set aside. In a large bowl, combine brownie mix and water. From into 1-inch balls. Dip into sugar mixture. Place on nonstick cookie sheet. Bake at 375° for 8 to 10 minutes.

Per Serving (1 cookie): Calories-65, Protein-.5 gm, Fat-0 gm, Carbohydrates- 16 gm, Cholesterol-0 mg, Sodium-80 mg.

SOFT MOLASSES COOKIES

⅔ *cup butter*

¾ *cup packed brown sugar*

⅓ *cup molasses*

1 egg

1 teaspoon vanilla extract

Preheat oven to 375°. In a 3 quart saucepan, melt butter over low heat. Add sugar, molasses, egg, and vanilla extract. Cook and stir over low heat until ingredients are well mixed. Space cookies 2 inches apart and drop by teaspoon onto ungreased cookie sheet. Bake at 375° for 7 to 9 minutes or until cookies are set. Do not overbake. Makes 3 dozen.

Per Serving (1 cookie): Calories-90, Protein-1 gm, Fat-3.5 gm, Carbohydrates-13 gm, Cholesterol-15 mg, Sodium-7 mg.

QUICK PRALINE COOKIES

24 graham cracker squares

½ cup packed brown sugar

½ cup margarine

½ teaspoon vanilla extract

½ cup chopped pecans

Super-Fast

Preheat oven to 350°. Arrange graham crackers in a single layer in a 15 x 10 x 1 inch jelly roll pan. Set aside. In a 2 quart saucepan, combine brown sugar and margarine. Cook and stir over medium heat, bring to a boil for one minute. Stir in vanilla extract. Evenly spread mixture over crackers. Sprinkle with pecans. Bake at 350° for 8 to 10 minutes. Cool before serving. Makes 2 dozen cookies.

Per Serving (1 cookie): Calories-95, Protein-0 gm, Fat-6 gm, Carbohydrates-10 gm, Cholesterol-0 mg, Sodium-90 mg.

• •

BUTTER GINGER SHORTBREAD

1 cup butter, softened

⅓ cup sugar

2 cups all-purpose flour

⅓ cup finely chopped crystallized ginger

1 tablespoon grated lemon peel

Glaze (see page 257)

Preheat oven to 325°. In a large bowl, using an electric mixer, cream butter and sugar until fluffy. Add flour, ginger, and lemon peel. Mix well. Shape dough into a ball; divide ball into 4 pieces. On an ungreased cookie sheet, flatten each piece to a six inch round. Press edges to smooth. Bake at 325° for 15 to 20 minutes or until edges are light golden brown. Cool on cookie sheet for 5 minutes. Drizzle glaze over wedges.

Glaze

½ cup confectioners' sugar

2 to 4 tablespoons fresh lemon juice

Combine sugar and lemon juice until smooth. Pour mixture into a resealable food storage bag. Cut off one corner of bag. Squeeze glaze onto cooled cookies.

Per Serving: Calories-100, Protein-1 gram, Fat-6 gm, Carbohydrates-11 gm, Cholesterol-15 mg, Sodium-60 mg.

• •

QUICK FIX CARAMEL BARS

Vegetable cooking spray

1 (14 ounce) package vanilla caramels

3 tablespoons milk

6 cups Cheerios®

2 cups dried apple rings, chopped

Coat a 9 inch square baking pan with vegetable cooking spray. Set aside. In a large Dutch oven, combine caramels and milk. Cook and stir over low heat until smooth. Remove from heat. Add Cheerios® and apple rings. Mix until evenly coated. Press mixture into prepared pan. Chill until firm. Cut into bars. Makes 9 bars.

Per Serving: Calories-280, Protein-5 gm, Fat-4.5 gm, Carbohydrates-57 gm, Cholesterol-5 mg, Sodium-290 mg.

CREATE A QUICK FROSTING BY PLACING A MARSHMALLOW ON TOP OF EACH CUPCAKE DURING THE LAST COUPLE OF MINUTES OF BAKING. .

CHOCOLATE PEANUT BARS

12 graham crackers

¾ cup packed brown sugar

¾ cup butter

1 (16 ounce) package semi-sweet real chocolate chips

1 cup salted cocktail peanuts

Super-Fast

Line a 15 x 10 x 1 inch jelly roll pan with graham crackers. Set aside. In a 2 quart saucepan, combine sugar and butter. Cook and stir over medium heat until mixture boils. Cook for 4 minutes. Spread over graham crackers. Sprinkle with chocolate chips. Let stand 1 minute. Sprinkle with peanuts, lightly pressing into chocolate. Break into pieces. Makes 48 bars.

Per Serving (1 bar): Calories-100, Protein-1 gram, Fat-6 gm, Carbohydrates-11 gm, Cholesterol-10 mg, Sodium-110 mg.

HOMEMADE GRANOLA POWER BAR

Vegetable cooking spray

⅓ cup honey

¼ cup packed brown sugar

¼ cup butter

4 cups low-fat granola cereal

⅔ cup chunky peanut butter

¼ cup chocolate chips

2 teaspoons solid vegetable shortening

Coat a 9 inch square baking pan with non-stick vegetable cooking spray. Set aside. In a large saucepan, combine honey, sugar, and butter. Cook and stir over medium heat until mixture boils. Remove from heat. Add cereal and peanut butter. Press mixture into prepared pan. In a small saucepan, melt chocolate chips and vegetable shortening, stirring until smooth. Drizzle over bars. Chill until firm. Makes 16 bars.

Per Serving (1 bar): Calories-250, Protein-5 gm, Fat-11 gm, Carbohydrates-35 gm, Cholesterol-10 mg, Sodium-110 mg.

• •

JAM SNACK BARS

3 cups miniature marshmallows

1 cup plus 1 tablespoon crunchy peanut butter

½ cup butter

4½ cups rice cereal

⅔ cup strawberry jam

½ cup milk chocolate chips

2 teaspoons shortening

In a 3 quart saucepan, melt marshmallows, 1 cup of the peanut butter, and butter over low heat, stirring until smooth. Quickly stir in cereal, mixing until well coated. Press mixture into an ungreased 11 x 7 inch pan. Spoon jam over hot mixture. In a small saucepan, combine chocolate chips, 1 tablespoon of the peanut butter, and shortening. Cook and stir over low heat until well blended. Spread over jam. Chill until firm. Cut into bars. Makes 32 bars.

Per Serving (1 bar): Calories-140, Protein-3 gm, Fat-8 gm, Carbohydrates-14 gm, Cholesterol-10 mg, Sodium-110 mg.

EVENLY SLICE BAR COOKIES BY USING A PIZZA CUTTER.

CARAMEL APPLE BARS

1 (14 ounce) package vanilla caramels

3 tablespoons milk

6 cups toasted oat cereal

2 cups dried apple rings

In a 4-quart Dutch oven combine caramels and milk. Cook over low hear, stirring until smooth. Remove pan from heat. Add cereal and apple rings to caramel mixture and mix until evenly coated. Press mixture into greased 9 x 9 x 2 inch pan. Chill until firm. Cut into bars.

Per Serving (one bar): Calories-280, Protein-5 gm, Fat-4.5 gm, Carbohydrates-57 gm, Cholesterol-5 mg, Sodium-220 mg.

• •

NO GUILT POUND CAKE

¾ cup all-purpose flour

1½ teaspoons baking powder

¼ cup unsalted margarine

¼ cup sugar

2 eggs

2 teaspoons vanilla extract

Preheat oven to 350°. Coat a 7 x 4 x 2 inch loaf pan with vegetable cooking spray. Set aside. In a small bowl, sift flour and baking powder. Set aside. In a medium bowl, using an electric mixer, cream margarine, gradually adding sugar. Beat until fluffy. Add eggs, one at a time, mixing thoroughly after each addition. Add vanilla extract. Gradually add dry ingredients, mixing until well blended. Pour mixture into prepared loaf pan. Bake 30 minutes or until golden brown. Makes 8 servings.

Per Serving: Calories-249, Protein-7 gm, Fat-8 gm, Carbohydrates-37 gm, Cholesterol-70 mg, Sodium-165 mg.

FANCY ANGEL FOOD CAKE

2½ cups sliced strawberries, divided

2 teaspoons sugar

2 tablespoons raspberry blend juice

1 (9 ounce) prepared angel food cake

1 (12 ounce) container frozen whipped topping, thawed

Super-Fast

In a medium bowl, combine berries, sugar, and juice. Set aside. Cut cake in half horizontally. Spoon half the berry mixture over bottom half of cake. Top with remaining half of cake. Spread with remaining berries.Cover cake with frozen topping. Chill before serving. Makes 8 servings.

Per Serving: Calories-326, Protein-4 gm, Fat-7 gm, Carbohydrates-55 gm, Cholesterol-0 mg, Sodium-40 mg.

COCONUT FRUIT DESSERT

1 small orange

1 cup honeydew melon balls

1 banana, sliced

1 teaspoon lemon juice

½ teaspoon almond extract

1½ tablespoons shredded coconut, toasted

Remove skin and membrane from orange. Section orange into a medium bowl. Add melon balls, banana, lemon juice, and almond extract. Toss gently. Divide into 4 dessert dishes. Sprinkle with coconut. Chill.

Per Serving: Calories-65, Protein-1 gm, Fat-1 gm, Carbohydrates-15 gm, Cholesterol-0 mg, Sodium-6 mg.

BLUEBERRY FRUIT DESSERT

1 cup blueberries

2 tablespoons apple juice

½ teaspoon vanilla extract

1 cup non-fat vanilla yogurt

In a blender, combine blueberries, apple juice, and vanilla extract. Add yogurt and pulse until thoroughly blended. Chill before serving. Makes 2 servings.

Per Serving: Calories-133, Protein-7 gm, Fat-trace, Carbohydrates-25 gm, Cholesterol-2 mg, Sodium-88 mg.

• •

SWEET CHERRIES DESSERT

Vegetable cooking spray

2 cups pitted dark sweet cherries

3 eggs

1 cup milk

½ cup flour

¼ cup sugar

1 teaspoon vanilla extract

Confectioners' sugar

Preheat oven to 350°. Coat an 8 x 8 x 2 inch baking dish with nonstick spray. Pour cherries into baking dish. Set aside. In a large bowl, combine eggs, milk, flour, sugar, and vanilla extract. Use an electric mixer and beat until smooth. Spread mixture over cherries. Bake at 350° for 45 to 50 minutes or until puffed and golden brown. Sprinkle with confectioners' sugar before serving. Makes 6 servings.

Per Serving: Calories-170, Protein-6 gm, Fat-4 gm, Carbohydrates-29 gm, Cholesterol-110 mg, Sodium-50 mg.

HOMESPUN BLUEBERRY CRISPS

1 lemon

2 tablespoons brown sugar

2 teaspoons cornstarch

2 teaspoons almond-flavored liqueur

½ cup cold water

1 tablespoon butter

2½ cups blueberries

10 amaretto cookies, crushed

Confectioner's sugar

From lemon, grate ¼ teaspoon peel and squeeze 1 teaspoon juice. In a 2 quart saucepan, combine lemon peel, juice, brown sugar, cornstarch, almond liqueur, and water. Add butter and half the blueberries. Lightly crush blueberries with side of spoon. Cook and stir over medium heat until mixture boils. Add remaining blueberries and boil 2 minutes. Stir constantly. Spoon mixture into 4 dessert cups. Top with cookie crumbs and confectioner's sugar. Serve warm. Makes 4 servings.

Per Serving: Calories-160, Protein-1 gram, Fat-4 gm, Carbohydrates-30 gm, Cholesterol-0 mg, Sodium-50 mg.

TO KEEP BOILED SYRUP FROM CRYSTALLIZING, ADD A PINCH OF BAKING SODA TO THE CONTAINER.

SAUCY BERRY RHUBARB

1 (16 ounce) package frozen rhubarb, thawed

½ cup apple juice

3 tablespoons packed brown sugar

2 cups raspberries

2 tablespoons reduced-fat sour cream

In a 1 quart saucepan, combine rhubarb, juice, brown sugar, and 1 cup of the raspberries. Heat to boiling. Reduce heat. Simmer uncovered 10 minutes, stirring occasionally. Fold in remaining raspberries. Spoon into dessert dishes. Top with sour cream. Makes 6 servings.

Per Serving: Calories-72, Protein-1 gram, Fat-0 gm, Carbohy-drates-17 gm, Cholesterol-0 mg, Sodium-10 mg.

APPLESAUCE FOR ONE

1 small apple, cored, pared, and chopped

1 tablespoon lemon juice

3 packets sugar substitute

⅛ teaspoon cinnamon

Combine apples and lemon juice in a blender. Process until smooth. Add sugar substitute and cinnamon. Pulse until mixed. Pour into a small serving dish. Cover and chill before serving. Makes 1 serving.

Per Serving: Calories-62, Protein-0.2 gm, Fat-0.4 gm, Carbohy-drates-20 gm, Cholesterol-0 mg, Sodium-11 mg.

APRICOT YOGURT SUNDAE

1 (15 ounce) can reduced-sugar apricot halves

⅓ cup plus 2 tablespoons orange juice, divided

1 teaspoon brown sugar

1½ teaspoons cornstarch

1 teaspoon vanilla extract

2 cups fat-free vanilla yogurt

Drain apricots, reserving juice. Slice apricots. Set aside. In a medium saucepan, combine ⅓ cup of the orange juice, brown sugar, and reserved apricot juice. Bring to a boil. Reduce heat, simmer uncovered for 10 minutes. In a small bowl, combine cornstarch and remaining orange juice, stirring until smooth. Add to apricot mixture. Bring to a boil. Cook and stir for 2 minutes or until mixture thickens. Add vanilla extract and apricots. Serve over fat-free frozen yogurt. Makes 4 servings.

Per Serving: Calories-151, Protein-5 gm, Fat-trace, Carbohydrates-33 gm, Cholesterol-0 mg, Sodium-84 mg.

WALNUT CAKE SQUARES

6 tablespoons sifted cake flour

2 teaspoons baking powder

¾ cup sugar

½ teaspoon salt

1 cup chopped nuts

½ pound chopped dates

4 eggs

1 teaspoon vanilla

Confectioner's sugar

Preheat oven to 350 degrees. In a large bowl, combine flour and baking powder. Add sugar, salt, nuts and dates. Mix well. Add eggs one at a time, stirring after each addition. Add vanilla. Pour mixture into a greased and floured 9 x 9 inch baking pan. Bake for 30 minutes. Cut into squares while still warm and sprinkle with confectioner's sugar. Makes 9 servings.

Per Serving: Calories-275, Protein-6 gms, Fat-11 gm, Carbohydrates-4 gm, Cholesterol-04 mg, Sodium-247 mg.

TO KEEP BROWN SUGAR AND MARSHMALLOWS FROM BECOMING HARD OR STALE, STORE THEM IN THE FREEZER.

CRUNCHY CEREAL CLUSTERS

Vegetable cooking spray

½ cup butter

⅔ cup packed brown sugar

1 tablespoon light corn syrup

¼ teaspoon vanilla extract

3 cups crisp corn cereal squares

1 cup lightly salted cashews

Coat two cookie sheets with vegetable cooking spray. Set aside. In a 3 quart saucepan, melt butter. Add brown sugar and corn syrup. Bring mixture to a full boil, stirring constantly for 2 to 3 minutes. Remove from heat. Stir in vanilla extract, cereal, and cashews. Mix gently until cereal is coated. Drop by rounded tablespoons onto prepared cookie sheets. Cool. Makes 24 clusters.

Per Serving (1 cluster): Calories-100, Protein-1 gm, Fat-6 gm, Carbohydrates-11 gm, Cholesterol-10 mg, Sodium-105 mg.

• •

HOMEMADE CHOCOLATE FUDGE

1 (16 ounces) package semisweet chocolate

1 (14 ounces) sweetened condensed milk

1 cup chopped walnuts

1 teaspoon vanilla

Line an 8-inch square baking pan with plastic wrap. In a 2-quart saucepan, melt chocolate with condensed milk over medium-low heat, stirring until smooth. Remove from heat. Stir in walnuts and vanilla. Pour mixture into baking pan, spread evenly. Chill until firm. Cut into 64 pieces.

Per Serving (1 piece): Calories-67, Protein-1 gm, Fat-4 gm, Carbohydrates 8-gm, cholesterol 2-mg, sodium 13-mg.

SWEET AND COOL PEPPERMINTS

3¼ to 4 cups confectioners' sugar

⅔ cup sweetened condensed milk

Red food coloring

½ teaspoon peppermint extract

Line a cookie sheet with waxed paper and set aside. In a medium bowl, combine sugar, milk, and a few drops of red food coloring. Add extract and enough additional sugar to make a smooth, creamy mixture. Shape into 1 inch balls. Place balls on cookie sheet. Using a fork, flatten each ball to ¼ inch thickness. Let stand, uncovered, at room temperature for 1 hour. Turn candies over and let stand an additional hour. Store mints in air-tight containers. Makes 7½ dozen.

Per Serving (1 mint): Calories-25, Protein-0 gm, Fat-0 gm, Carbohydrates-6 gm, Cholesterol-0 mg, Sodium-5 mg.

Index

OTHER COOKBOOKS NOW AVAILABLE

To order, fill out enclosed order form.

BUSY WOMAN'S COOKBOOK A national bestseller by Sharon and Gene McFall Over 350,000 copies sold. It has over 500 mouth-watering 3 and 4 ingredient recipes and more than 200 short stories and facts about famous and influential women. $16.95

COOKIN' WITH WILL ROGERS by Sharon and Gene McFall. Has over 560 delicious country cookin' recipes with over 100 Will Rogers quotes, 60 pictures and 50 stories of one of America's most beloved humorists. "Only a fool argues with a skunk, a mule or a cook." Will Rogers. $19.95.

HOME MADE BLESSINGS by Diane Reasoner. Over 400 excellent tasting recipes, straight forward instructions and ingredients that are found in any pantry. Inspirational sayings on every page that will brighten your day. $19.95.

MILD TO WILD MEXICAN COOKBOOK by Linda Burgett. Over 400 tantalizing recipes from south of the border. Every recipe tells you if it is hot, medium or mild-so you have no big surprises. Also has fun facts on ingredients. One word for this book—Wonderful. $18.95.

JUST AROUND THE CURVE by Sharon and Gene McFall. Designed for RVers and Campers, but is great for the home. Over 350 great quick and easy recipes. Recipes from all 50 states. Also contains some low-fat, low-cal and diabetic recipes. Intriguing American points of interest and travel tips and tidbits. A must for the traveler or at home. $16.95.

COMING SOON

IF I GOTTA COOK MAKE IT QUICK by Shelley Plettl. Over 500 delicious crockpot and just a few ingredients recipes. Includes: Helpful Hints and Fun Facts; How to Adapt Your Favorite Recipe to the Crockpot; How to Substitute One Ingredient for Another; Uses of Herbs and Spices; Basic Rules for Table Manners. $18.95

Please send _____ copies of_____

@ _____ (U.S.) each $_____

Postage and handling @ $3.50 each $_____

Texas residents add sales tax @ $1.69 each $_____

TOTAL $_____

Check or Credit Card (Canada-credit card only)

Charge to my ☐ Master Card or Visa Card

account # _____

expiration date _____

signature _____

MAIL TO:
Creative Ideas Publishing
7916 N.W. 23rd St.
P.M.B. 115
Bethany, OK 73003-5135

Name _____

Address _____

City _____ _____ State _____ Zip _____

Phone (day) _____ (night) ____ _____

ORDER BY EMAIL: sharoncookin@aol.com

Please send _____ copies of *Get me out of the Kitchen!*

@ $18.95 (U.S.) each $_____

Postage and handling @ $3.50 each $_____

Texas residents add sales tax @ $1.69 each $_____

TOTAL $_____

Check or Credit Card (Canada-credit card only)

Charge to my ☐ Master Card or Visa Card

account # _____

expiration date _____

signature _____

MAIL TO:
Creative Ideas Publishing
7916 N.W. 23rd St.
P.M.B. 115
Bethany, OK 73003-5135

Name _____

Address _____

City _____ State _____ Zip _____

Phone (day) _____ (night) _____

ORDER BY EMAIL: sharoncookin@aol.com

SHARE YOUR FAVORITE RECIPE

Do you have a favorite quick and easy recipe? Do family and friends ask you for it? Would you like to see it in a national cookbook?

If so, lease send your favorite quick and easy recipe to us. If we use it in a future cookbook, you will be given credit in the book for the recipe, and will receive a free copy of the book.

Submit to: Creative Ideas Publishing
PMB 115
7916 N.W. 23rd Street
Bethany, OK 73003-5135